CRAFT AND ART

SILK SCREEN PRINTING

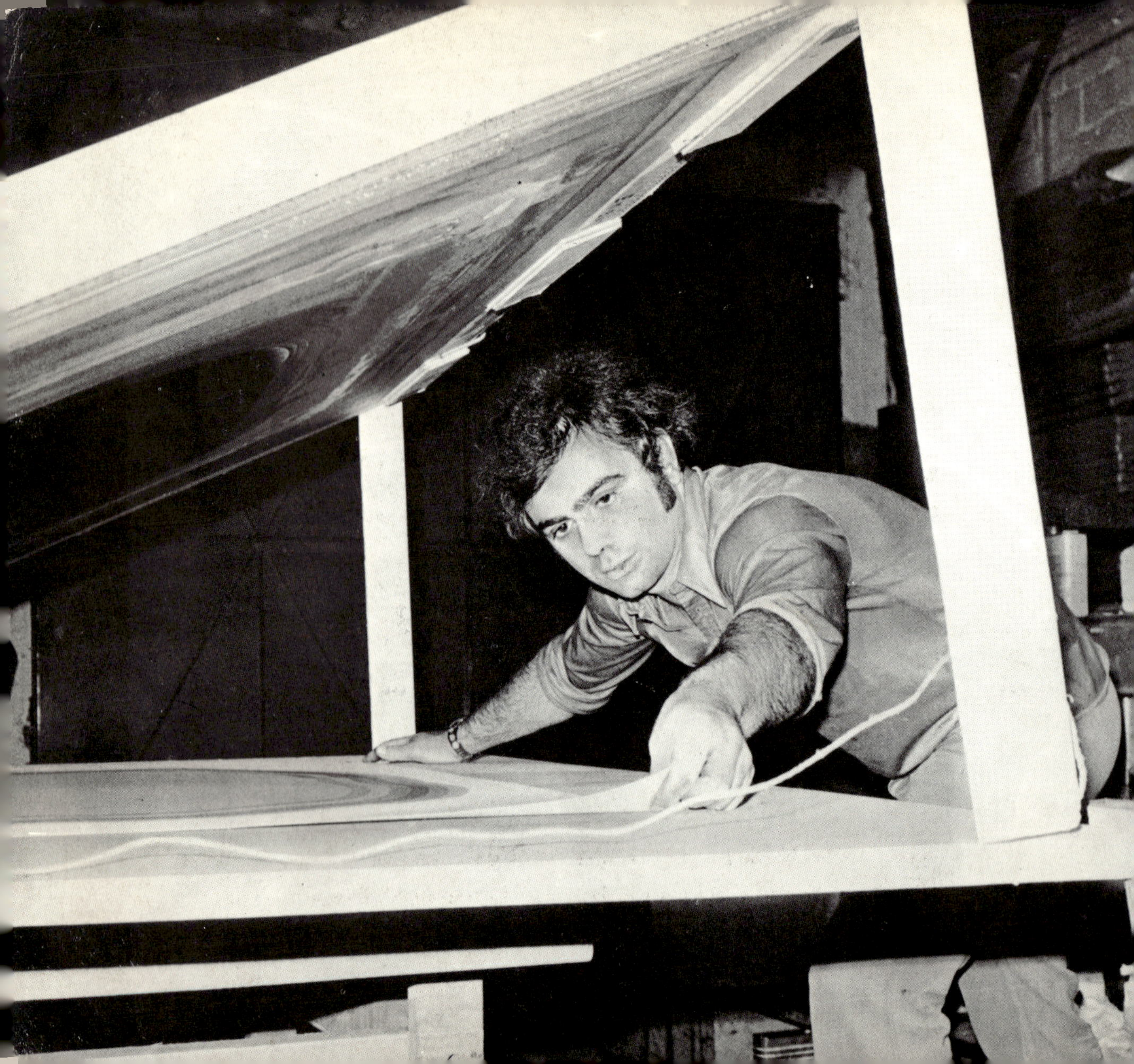

CRAFT AND ART

Michel Caza

SILK SCREEN PRINTING

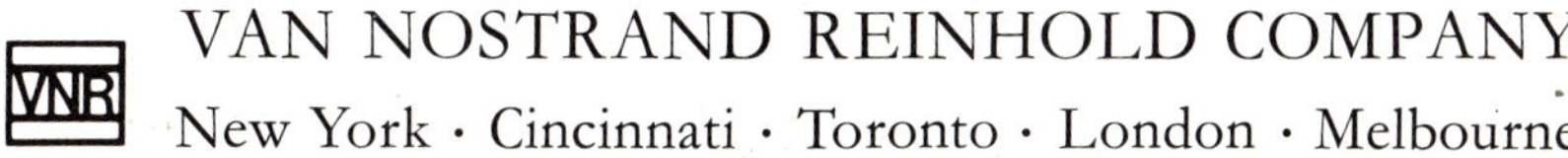

VNR VAN NOSTRAND REINHOLD COMPANY
New York · Cincinnati · Toronto · London · Melbourne

Library of Congress Catalog Card No.: 73-8469
ISBN 0-442-29992-3

Printed in Switzerland.

Published in 1974 by Van Nostrand Reinhold Company Inc., 450 West 33rd Street, New York N.Y. 10001 and Van Nostrand Reinhold Company Ltd., 25–28 Buckingham Gate, London SW1E 6LQ.

Van Nostrand Reinhold Company Regional Offices:
New York, Cincinnati, Chicago, Millbrae, Dallas.
Van Nostrand Reinhold Company International Offices:
London, Toronto, Melbourne.

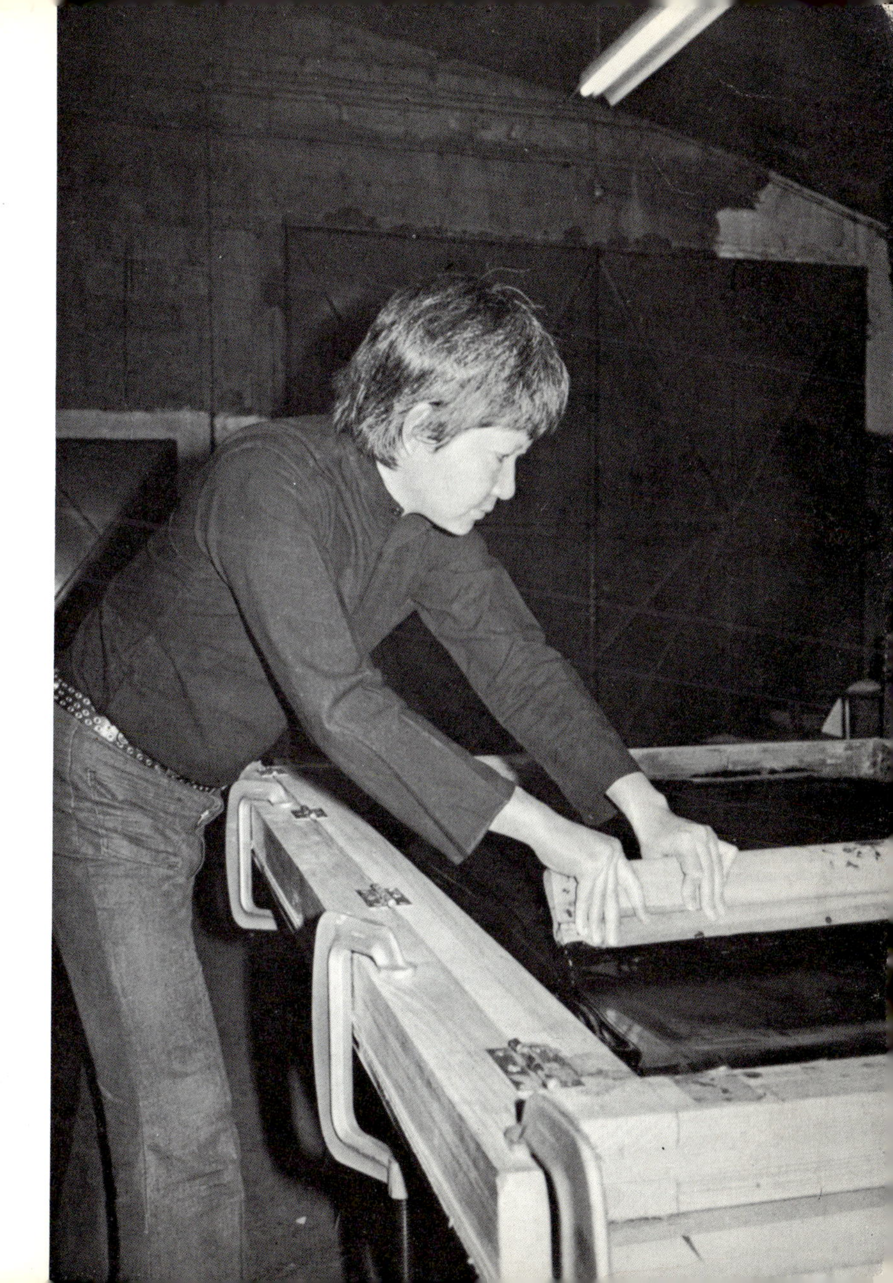

CONTENTS

1 INK THROUGH MESH 9

2 THE SCREEN 17
The fabric
Origins
Natural silk
Nylon
Terylene
Choice of fabric
The frame and the stretching of the fabric
Preparing the fabric

3 WORKING DIRECTLY ON THE SCREEN 27
Line work and flat colour
Block-out
Drawing with "seroid"
Drawing with litho ink
Nylogravure
The Mercier method
Half-tones
Litho crayon

4 WORKING INDIRECTLY AWAY FROM THE SCREEN 39
Hand-cut stencil papers
Photochemical techniques
Making the transparent positive
Hand-made transparent positive
Brush work
Hand-cut transparent positives
Engraved transparent positives
Working with litho crayon
Photographic transparent positives
The Linstead mixed method

5 PRINTING 59
What to print on?
Paper
Other materials
Ink

Superimposed transparent inks
The printing table
The hand press
The squeegee
Registration and maintaining registration
Clearance
How to print
Possible printing mishaps
Drying
Cleaning and recuperating the screen

6 THE ARTIST AND THE SCREEN PRINTER 78

7 VARIATIONS 81

8 SILK SCREEN IN ADVERTISING, DECORATION AND INDUSTRY 85

9 THE HISTORY OF SILK SCREEN 94

10 FOR COLLECTORS 107
An "original screen print"
An "original silk screen copy"
A "screen print reproduction"
Signing and numbering
Trial proofs
States
Over-proofs
Artist's proofs

GLOSSARY OF TECHNICAL TERMS 114

SELECT BIBLIOGRAPHY 118

TABLE OF ILLUSTRATIONS 119

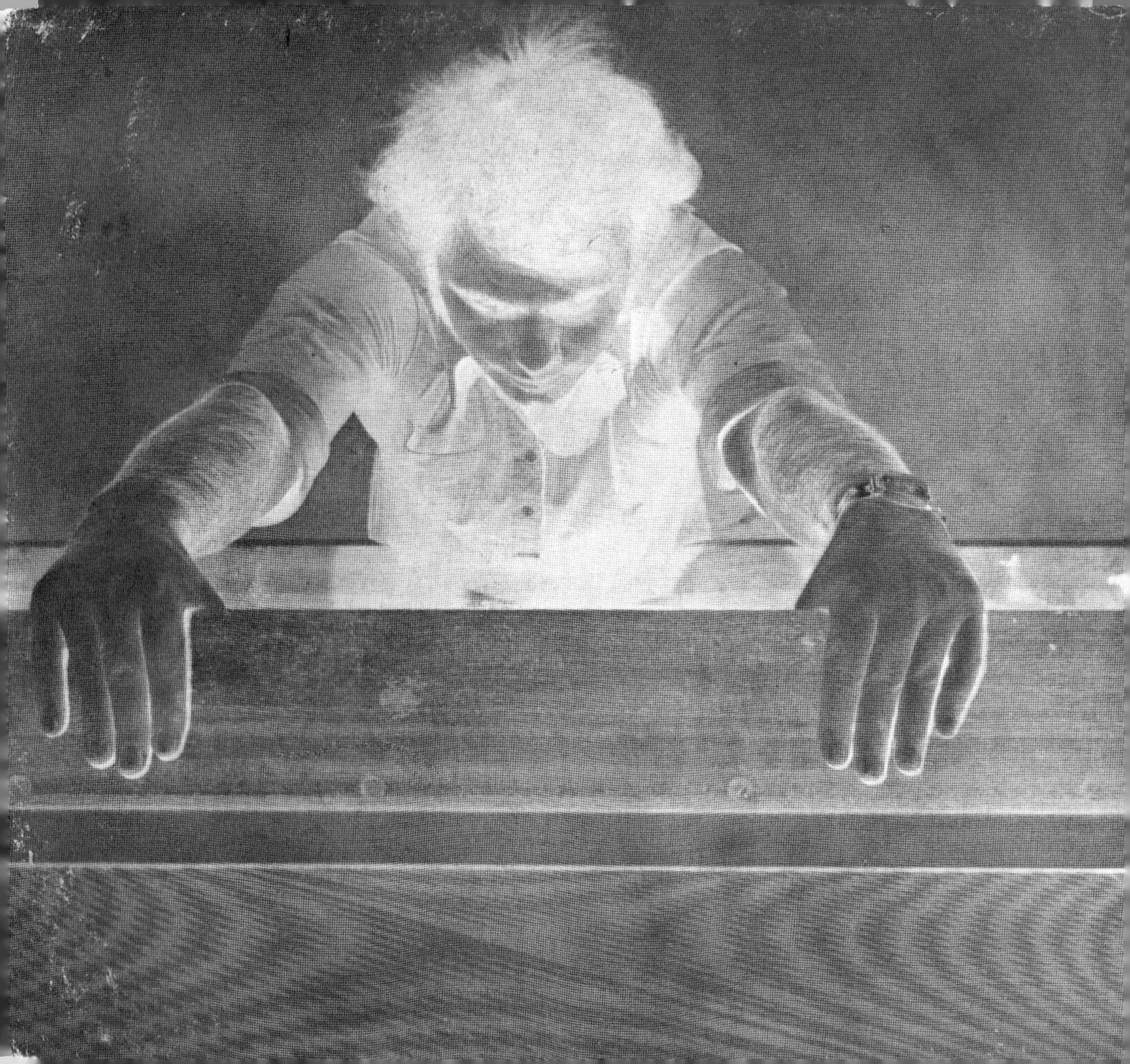

1 INK THROUGH MESH

Silk screen printing, or serigraphy, is a field or artistic expression where intense activity has been taking place these last few years and which is still developing rapidly. Long considered a "minor" technique, for reasons hard to understand, it has only recently become "respectable" in Europe thanks to the efforts of enthusiastic young artists who have found it an ideal means of expression. This is astonishing to American artists who have been expressing themselves "serigraphically" for fifty years or so, and in all styles, from figurative work to pop art.

Being a "quick" technique calling for little heavy material while permitting considerable variations of pictorial style, from flat colours to half-tones, silk screen is ideally suited to a society like ours, torn between frenzied industrialisation and the rage to live at an ever faster pace in ever greater comfort.

Is it a coincidence or a sign of the times that silk screen printing should be so akin in spirit to many other modern pictorial techniques? Scores of young artists, whether they be cinetic, pop or op, structuralist, perspectivist, constructivist, etc., find in it the precision, vigorous colouring and tone density which suit their styles. And the public's growing taste for prints has now raised silk screen to the status of full member in the graphic techniques club.

The author does not intend this book to be a complete and complicated technical manual; he proposes merely to help artists and art-lovers to familiarize themselves quickly but in some depth with the possibilities of silk screen printing. A short bibliography and a glossary of technical terms will assist the reader in carrying his knowledge further.

Working directly on the screen

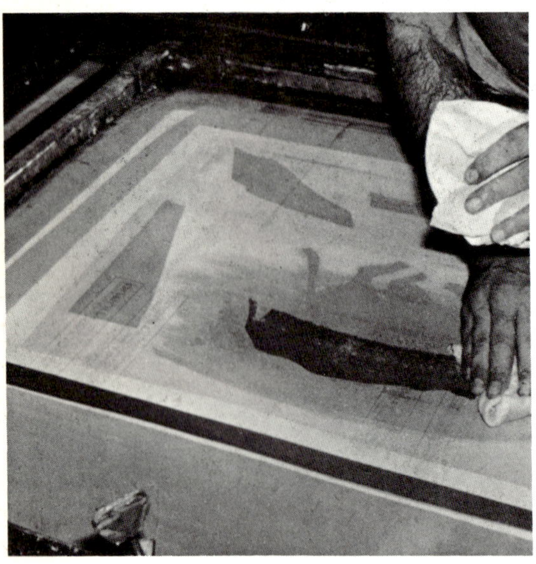

The origins of silk screen can be traced back to the very ancient technique of stencilling; for stencilling, unlike lithography or engraving, is a process where ink passes *through* the printing surface instead of being transferred *from* it to the paper. The printing surface here consists of an extremely fine mesh stretched on a frame: the *screen*. This screen, which is partially blocked out and made impermeable by manual or photochemical means, is only left unobstructed in those areas where the artist intends the ink to pass through the mesh. Ink is poured onto the upper surface of the screen, then forced through it with a rubber blade held by a handle, called the squeegee. Where it meets with no obstruction the ink passes through the screen and thus

What comes first is the screen

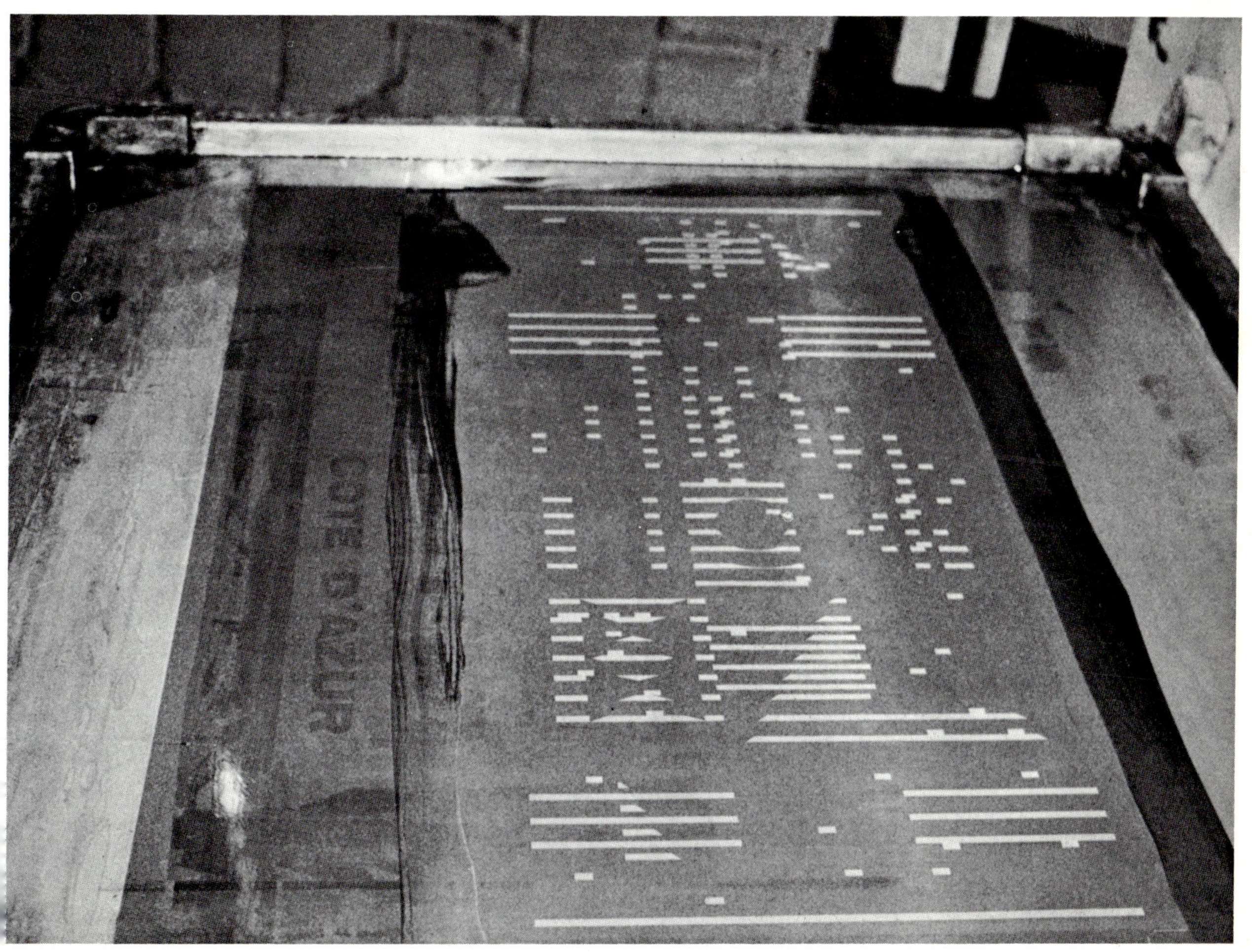
COTE D'AZUR

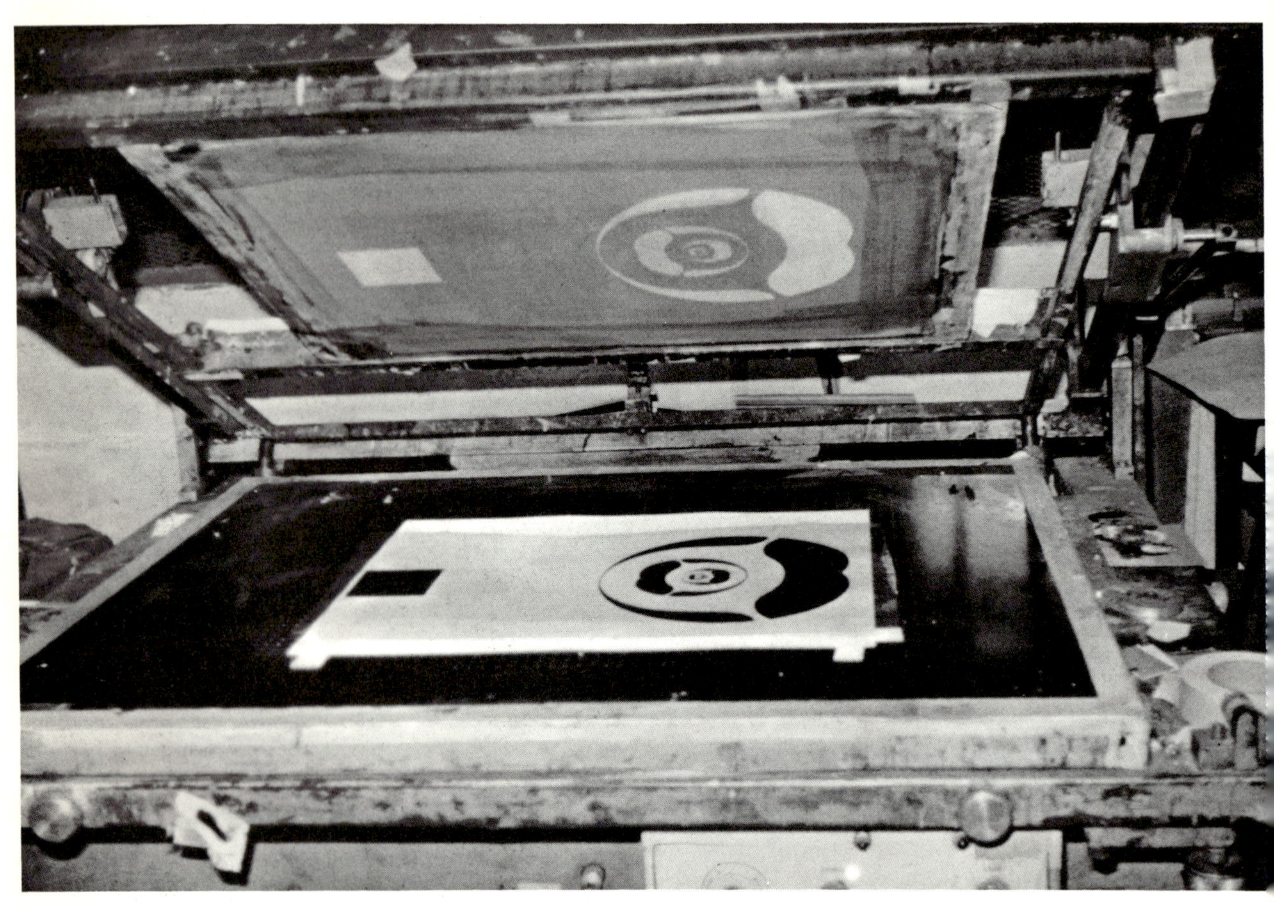

The base and the screen

covers the sheet of paper, previously placed underneath, exactly as intended by the artist. The fact that the ink goes *through a screen* instead of being applied directly makes it possible to print on a great variety of surfaces of almost any form.

Versatility is therefore one of the major characteristics of silk screen printing; it can be applied to a great many tasks, not only in art and graphics, but also in industry and decoration.

Another important feature of silk screen is that it can attain an almost unrivalled intensity of colour. Also, light colours can successfully be superimposed on dark colours, or fluorescent ink used, as is done by so many contemporary artists. All this is made possible by the relative thickness of the layer of ink.

In this book we shall deal mainly with Art silk screen, and more particularly with "original" silk screen printing, in which the artist prepares the stencil himself either by working directly on the screen

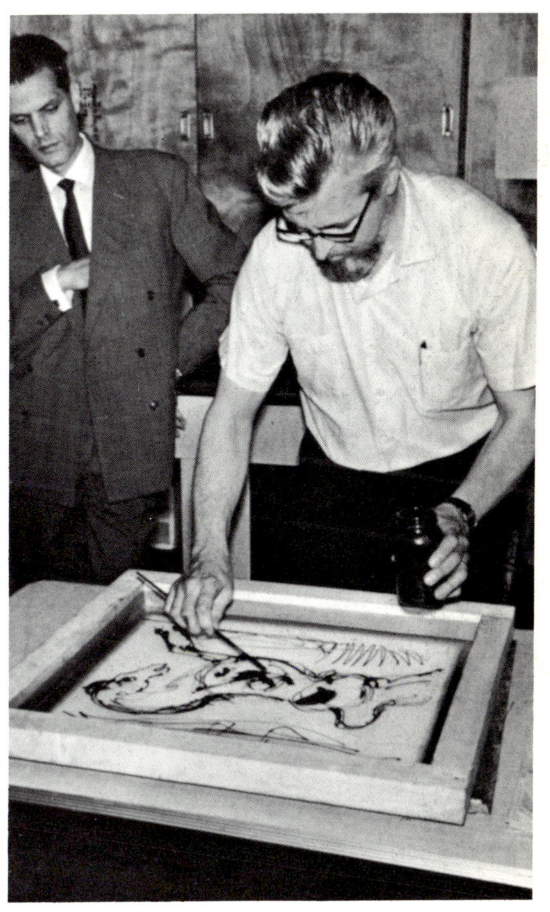

Dean Meeker working directly on the screen

by hand or by making a transparent positive which is then transferred photochemically to the screen by a silk screen printer. This "indirect" approach often permits the artist to introduce greater subtlety into his work, and when coupled with the full use of the various media and photographic effects—as in pop art, presents him with an incomparably rich range of expression.

In the more usual case of the artist not being himself a silk screen printer, he entrusts a professional with the actual business of printing, while closely supervising the stencil, the choice of colours and the quality of the print. A close, almost intimate collaboration must therefore develop between the artist and the printer. The latter, who becomes an active partner in the creation of the print, almost needs the qualities of a chameleon for he must be able to adapt himself as much as possible to the personal style of the artist in order to advise him on the choice of the right technique. Only in this way can he prevent the original work from becoming adulterated or ruined by technical mishaps. There are even extreme cases of what could be called "bicephalic" creation, in which the artist provides the basic graphic design and the printer looks after the colours. A print created this way could and should be signed by both its authors.

Joe Tilson, Earth, *1971. Silk screen and collage*

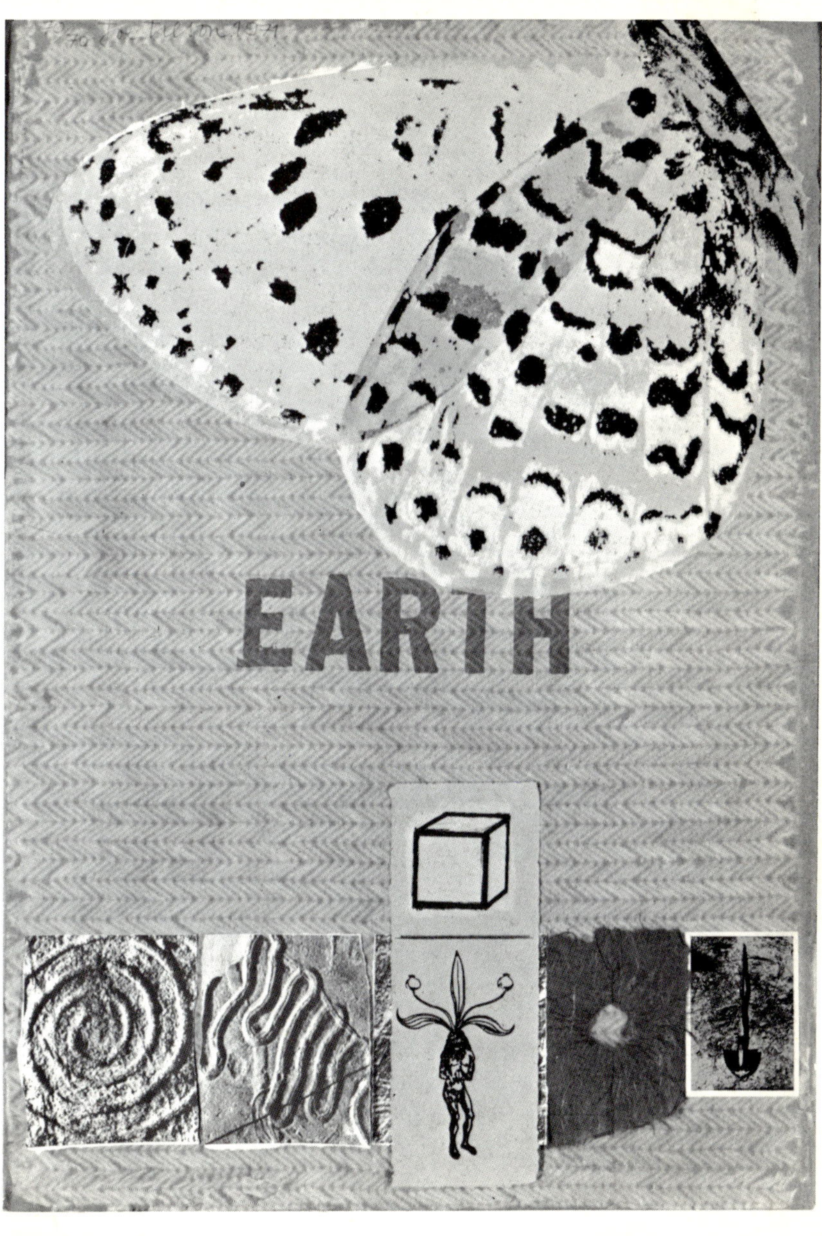
EARTH

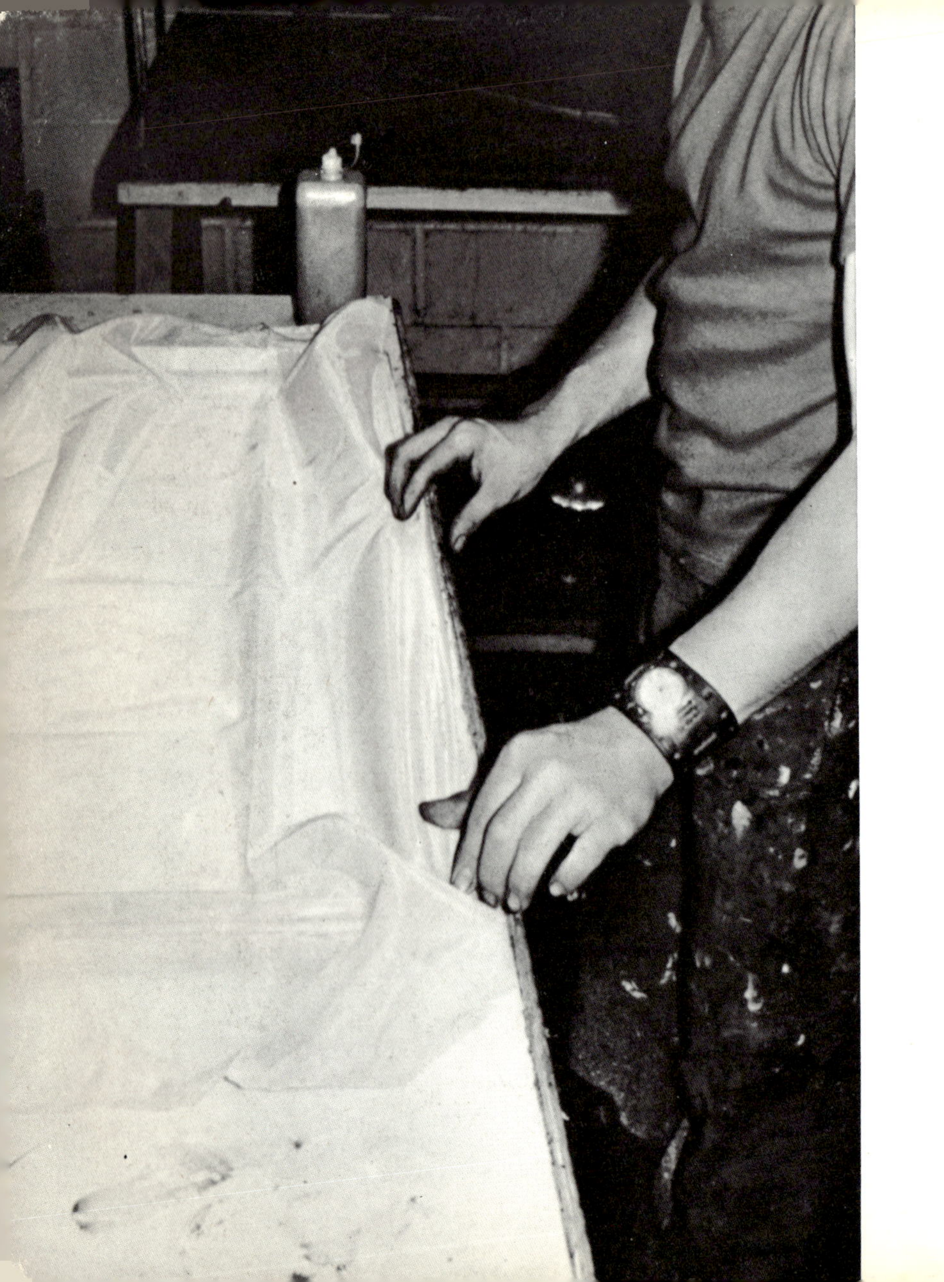

2 THE SCREEN

Without the screen, which supports and transmits the image, silk screen printing would not exist. The screen is a fabric woven exclusively for the purpose and stretched on a wood or metal frame.

The fabric

As the design is drawn directly on the fabric and ink passes through that part of the *mesh* which is left open, the choice and quality of the material are of the utmost importance.

Origins

Early this century organdie was used, but it is a fragile fabric and difficult to stretch; printers soon noticed that bolting silk used to sift flour produced better results. Hence the name "silk screen" or "serigraph". From 1930 onwards, manufacturers, sensing the growth of a potential market, started to weave printing silk to precise specifications. Synthetic fabrics appeared during the war, first nylon, then later, towards 1955, terylene. Metal mesh made from phosphor bronze or

Preparing the fabric on the screen

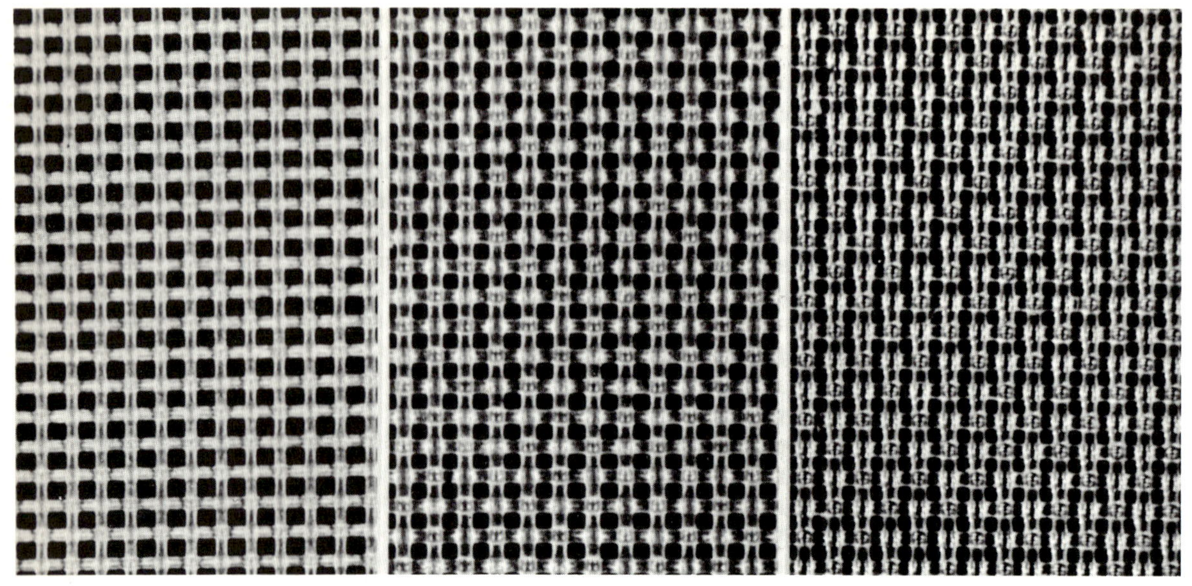

Three qualities of synthetic fibre fabric (light, medium, heavy)

stainless steel also came to be used in the industrial applications of silk screen printing.

These days, although silk is still the material traditionally used in the United States and in Great Britain, artists in the rest of the world tend to prefer man-made fabrics.

Natural silk

Composed of fibroin (76%), sericin (22%), wax and grease (1.70%) and sodium

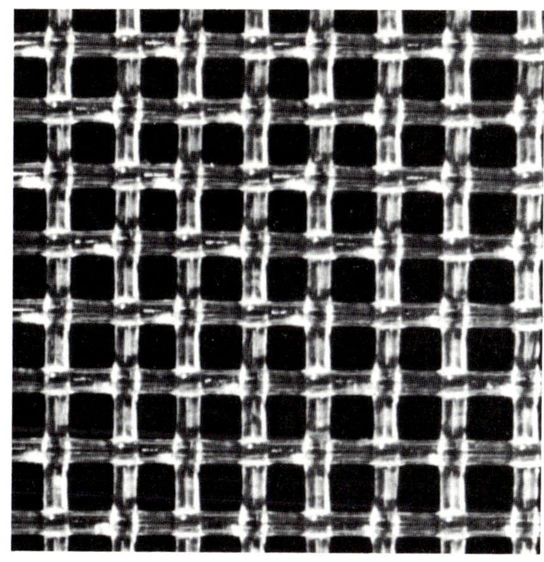

Detail of fabric magnified 50 times

chloride (0.30%), it resists nearly all solvents, but is attacked by acids and bases of more than 5% concentration. The various weaves are *taffeta* (plain square weave of warp and weft), *half-gauze* (threads interlocked at every other intersection), or *full-gauze* (threads interlocked at every intersection). Being a multifilament fabric it appears slightly rough. Silk is usually woven in various sizes, from 0000 (18 meshes to the square inch) to 25 (200 meshes to the square inch). There are four thicknesses of thread, standard (S), x, xx and xxx, which depend on the number of twists in the yarn. It should be stretched to about 2%.

Nylon

A synthetic polyamide with long molecular chains which resists all solvents, acids and bases. It is only vulnerable to strong concentrations of mineral acids. Nylon is supple and very strong, it should be stretched to 7%, its coefficient of extension being three times greater than that of silk; its mechanical strength is thus 30 times greater.

Nylon is a smooth monofilament thread, always with a *taffeta* weave of between 40 and 500 meshes to the inch, the latter producing 250,000 intersections and meshes to the square inch. It is woven with thick (HD), medium (T) and fine (S) thread; this, as we shall see later, controls the passage of the ink, and thus the thickness of the layer.

Terylene

A polyester slightly less resistant to chemical agents than nylon, but, on the other hand, less extensible (ideal tension 2%) and less sensitive to humidity in the air. It is a smooth monofilament with simply intersecting weave, which, like nylon, comes in a range of about thirty sizes, from 40 to 410 meshes to the inch in three thread thicknesses (HD, T, S).

Choice of fabric

From the above it is evident that there is a large range of fabrics to choose from. The artist must make his choice in relation to his intentions and means. Given equal quality in the weaving, we prefer terylene to nylon, the former being fractionally more stable. So the choice is really between silk and terylene. Schematizing a bit, in choosing a fabric there are five main points to take into consideration:

- The type of subject—for large flat areas of colour: fairly open weave, from 110 to 230 meshes to the inch; for fairly fine lines: medium weave, from 230 to 300 meshes to the inch; for fine work and half-tones: close weave, from 325 to 410 meshes to the inch.
- The artist's personal taste—when drawing directly on the screen he can choose between a rough (silk) surface and a smooth (terylene) surface.
- The intended thickness of the layer of ink—there are other factors but as a general rule open mesh leaves a thicker layer than close mesh.
- The surface that takes the print—any mesh for smooth paper (Bristol board, offset, art paper) and plastic; close mesh for rough paper (wove paper or vellum, rough litho, parchment, water colour).
- Wear (and therefore cost)—silk is fragile and more difficult to clean after stencilling and printing; terylene is easy to clean and use again. Barring accidents, it is almost indestructible.

Ronald Abram, Composition, *1970. 5 colour screen print*

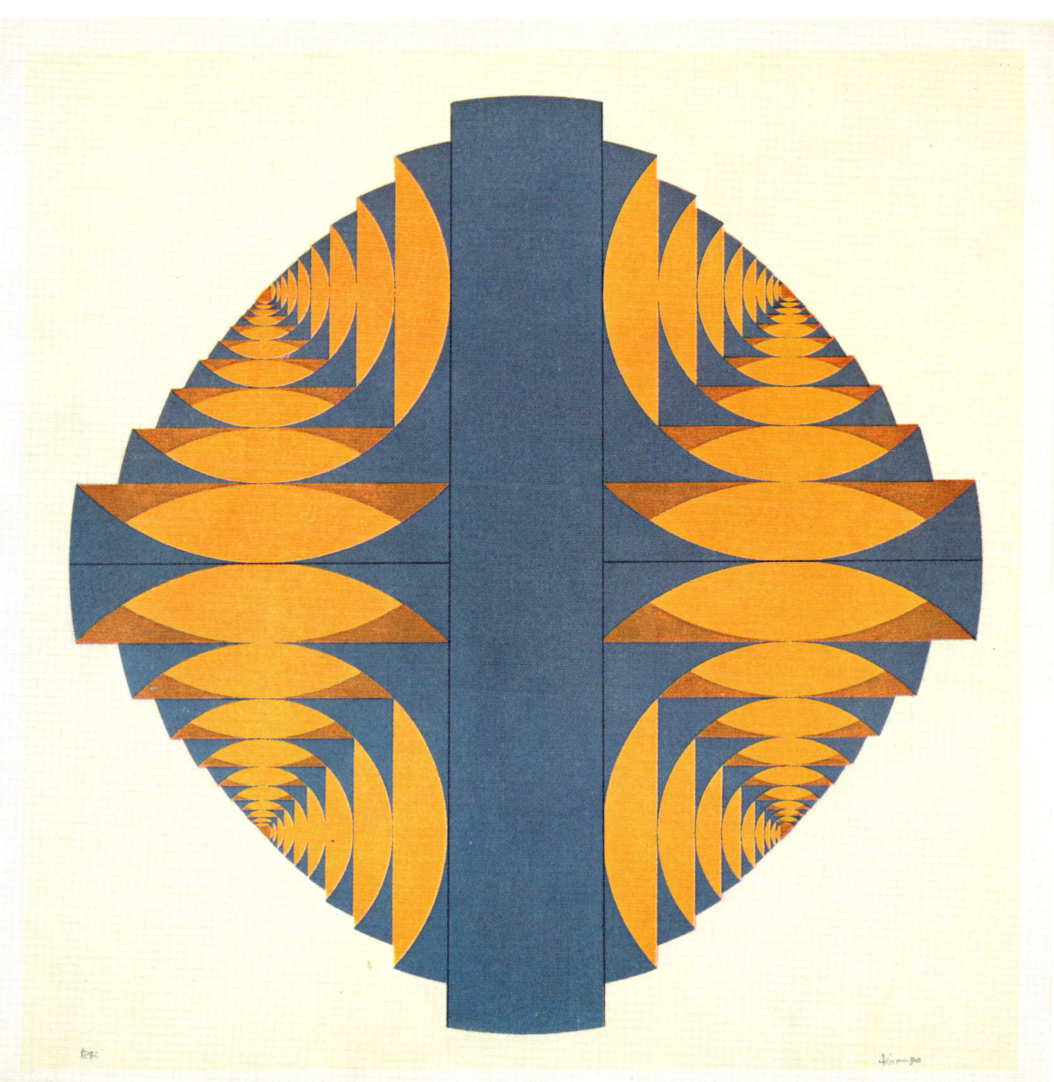

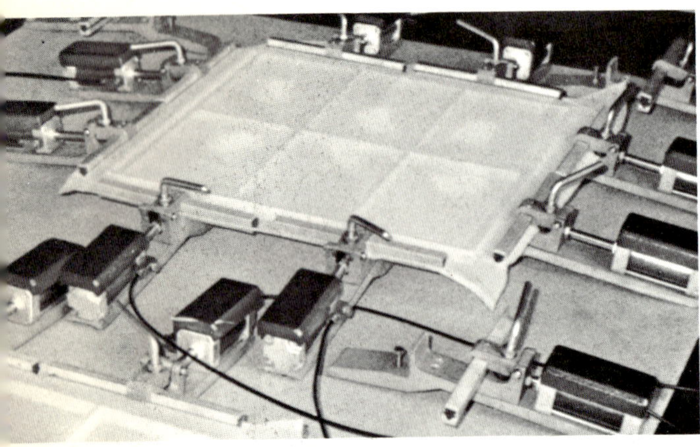

The fabric is stretched on a pneumatic machine, then glued to a metal frame

Manual stretching machine

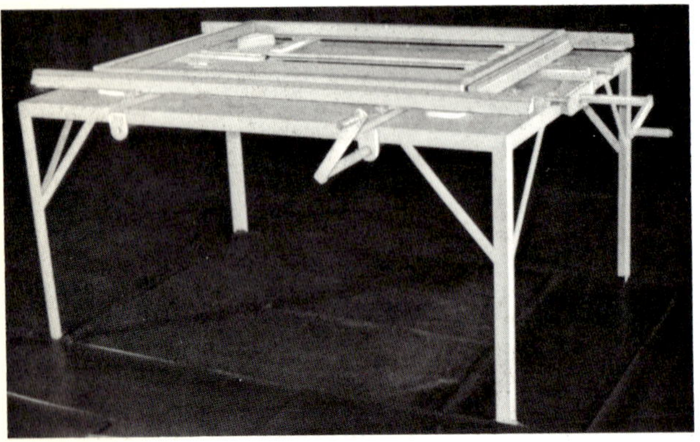

The frame and the stretching of the fabric

To set up a screen, the fabric must be tightly stretched on a frame. There are three sorts of frame: wood, to which the fabric is stapled, nailed or glued; metal, to which the fabric is glued; "self-stretchers", (the stretching mechanism is incorporated in the frame). This latter type, although relatively expensive, is very practical; it allows the printer to compensate, between successive applications of colour, for play in any direction by the paper receiving the image. If a wood frame is chosen, it is always better to buy one ready-made from a specialized supplier than to try and build one. For stretching, (in the absence of a self-stretching frame), the best results are obtained using mechanical or pneumatic stretching machines. This is costly equipment which only professionals and suppliers can afford. Still, it is possible to procure from a good supplier stretched

Fabric being stretched by hand on a wood frame

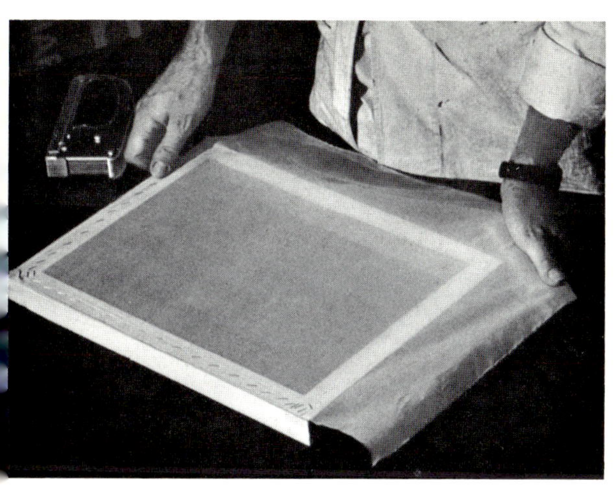

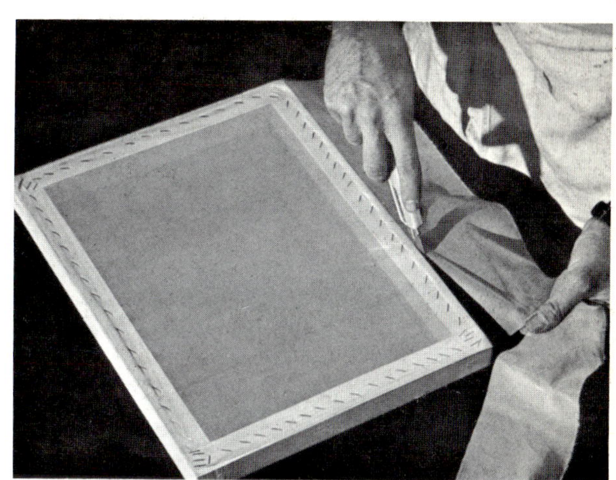

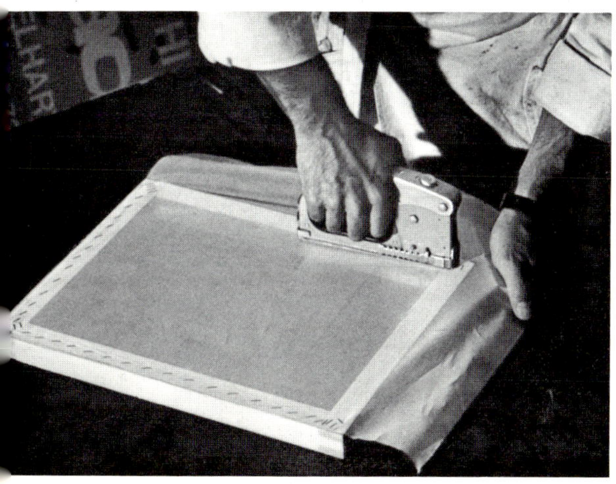

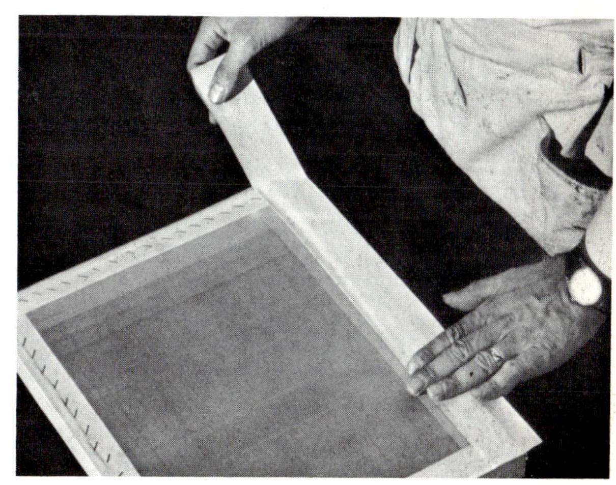

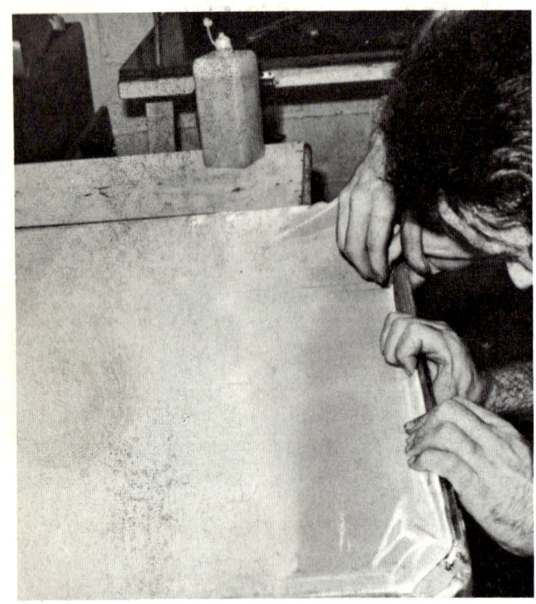

The fabric is fitted to the edges of a self-stretching frame

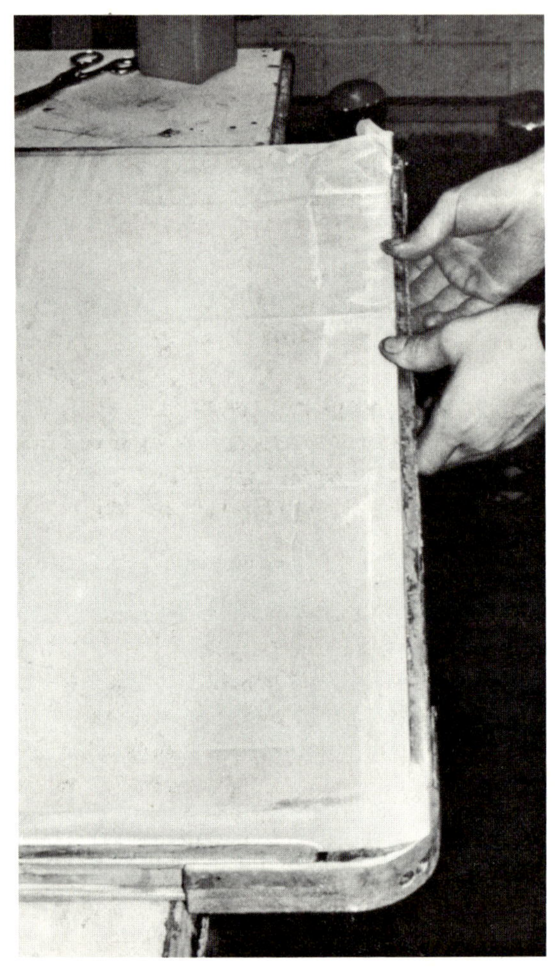

Self-stretching frame ready for stretching

frames of the desired size and fabric quality. The inside measurements of the screen must allow for a border of fabric about four inches greater all round than the dimensions of the image to be printed.

Preparing the fabric

Fabrics leaving the loom do not yet possess all the qualities that are indispensable for silk screen printing; silks always contain finishing products and greases, while terylene and nylon, because of their over-smooth threads prevent good adhesion of the image and good stencilling.

Silk

Once stretched, silk must be rubbed simultaneously on both sides with cloths impregnated with acetone or methyl ethyl ketone which are then evaporated by rubbing the fabric with a dry cloth. Next, the silk should be washed with a very weak tepid solution (2.5%) of sodium hypochlorite (industrial bleach), rinced thoroughly, then dried, with a fan if possible.

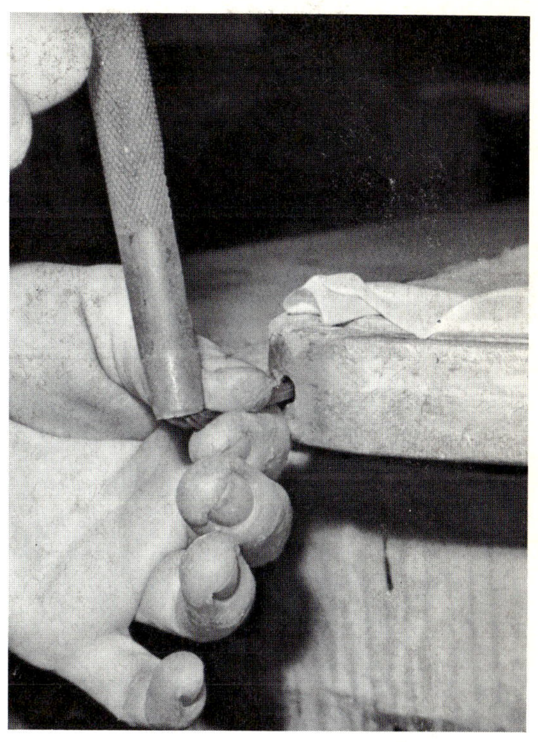

Stretching one corner of a self-stretching frame

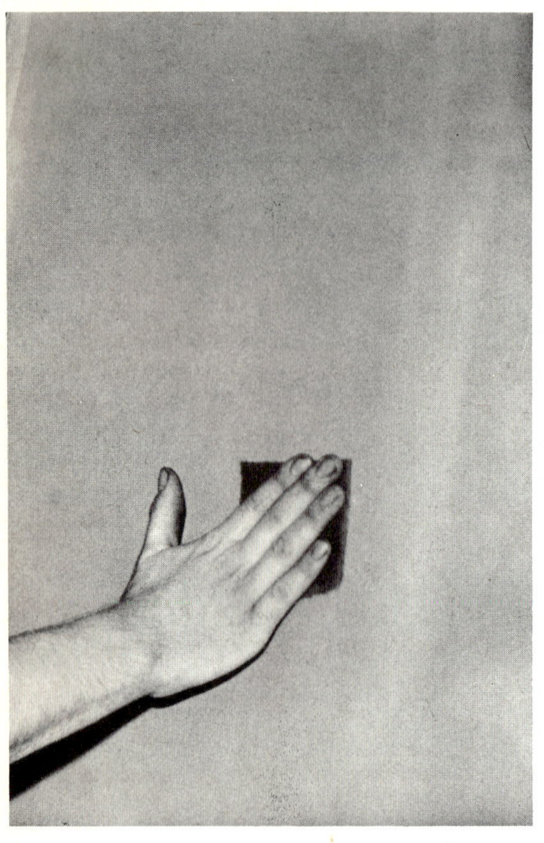

The fabric is prepared and degreased

Terylene and nylon

These must be both degreased and slightly roughened, particularly the under surface of the screen; a "mechanical" method is preferable to the chemical method often used. The whole of the lower surface must be rubbed gently but thoroughly for several minutes with a metallic sponge saturated in soap, using a continuous circular motion. The screen is then washed thoroughly in running water. Next, the artist (wearing rubber gloves) uses a plastic sponge to impregnate the screen with a concentrated solution (47·5 %) of sodium hypochlorite which he lets rest for 10 minutes, then rinces thoroughly and neutralizes with vinegar (weak acetic acid). The screen is rinced and dried. Whichever of these two materials is used, these operations are necessary for the screen to be ready to receive an image which it will transmit to the paper or, in other words, to be "stencilled".

3 WORKING DIRECTLY ON THE SCREEN

Whereas in lithography the techniques for drawing on and treating the stone are relatively few in number, in serigraphy there are many ways of preparing a screen for printing. As a rule, if an artist works directly on the screen he has a choice of five methods or combinations thereof, or else he can work on sheets of plastic or film which are later transferred to or under the screen by a chemical or photochemical process. In both cases the drawing is made the right way round, which is a great advantage for the artist. The inversion of the image which is unavoidable in lithography or in engraving, is not necessary in silk screen unless the artist should want the image to be printed on the back of a transparent plastic sheet and be seen through it.

Line work and flat colour. Block-out

This method, which is a favourite with American artists, consists in filling the mesh all around the image to be printed with a *block-out liquid* or *stopping-out medium*, usually a water-soluble base or cellulose which is applied with a brush. In this case the artist draws a "negative" image.

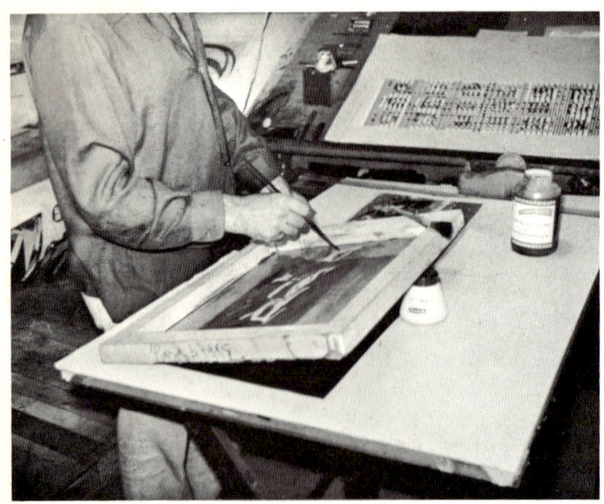

Drawing directly on the screen, "block-out"

A separate screen must be used for each colour conceived by the artist; "conceived" is an apt word, because by superimposing layers of transparent ink a multitude of new colours can be born on the print.

For direct drawing the screen can be placed directly on the *base* to which it is attached by hinges. This means that once the *guides* have been put in place (for the registration of the sheet of paper), the same screen can be used for each colour; the image merely needs to be effaced once printed, and a new one to be drawn in its place.

In *block-out* the artist starts by sketching in the contours of the image with a pencil, either directly, or by tracing over a sketch placed under the transparent screen. Parts of the mesh which are not meant to transmit ink are then filled by brush with block-out liquid. If the artist works with inks which are opaque and have good covering power, he may start by printing the largest areas, then, for each new colour, block out more and more of the screen. If he uses transparent inks he must allow for the effect of a previous layer of ink on a superimposed layer.

There are many different sorts of stopping-out liquid: glue size, shellac, gum lacquer, gum arabic and gelatine were used in the old days. Water-soluble unsensitized polyvinyl alcohol (P.V.A.) or tinted cellulose varnishes (soluble in acetone) are now more current. The former dries more slowly but is easier to use, precisely because it is a relatively slow

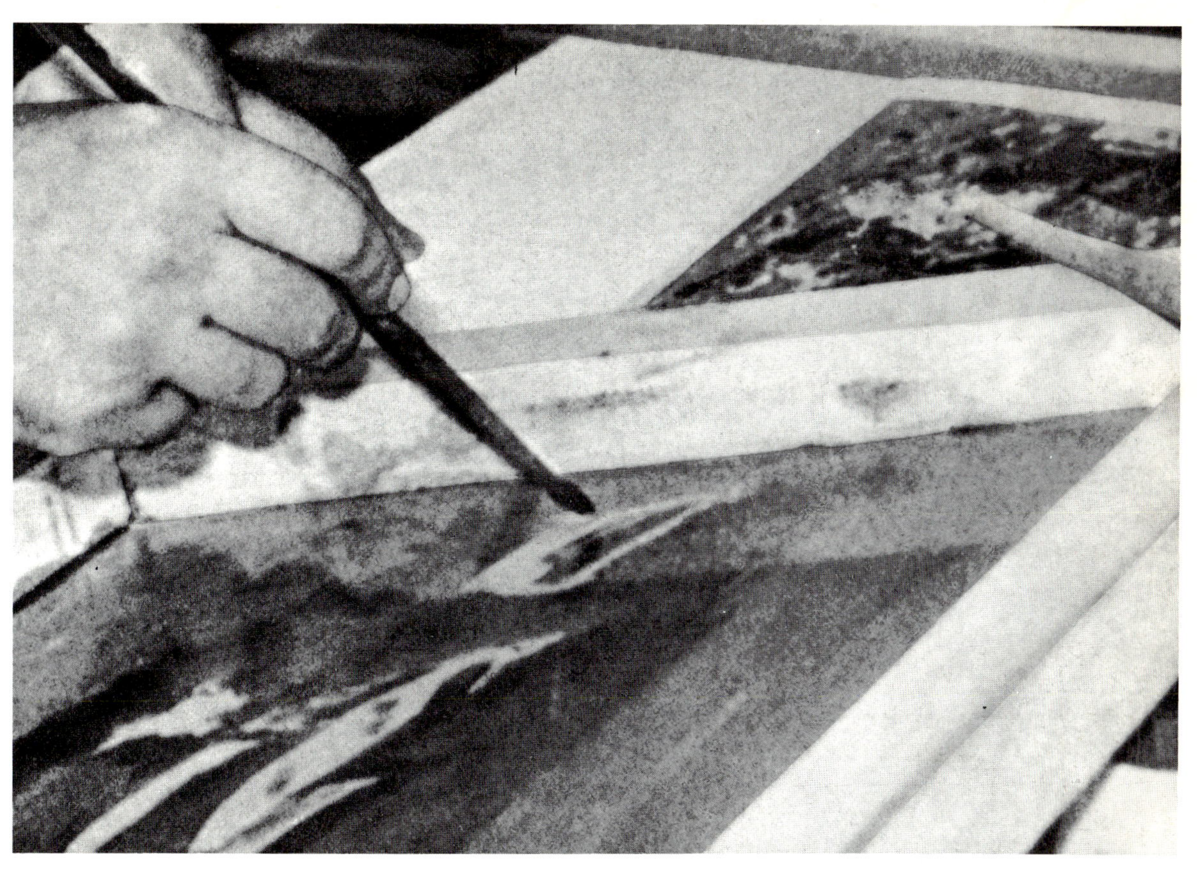

''Block-out''. The artist draws his composition directly on the screen the right way round

drier (15 min.). Cellulose varnishes dry in two minutes, but their evaporation can be slowed down by diluting them with heavy solvents like ethyl glycol.

Drawing with seroid

The technique described above has one major drawback: the image is produced by a "negative" method. It also greatly limits fine line work. Seroid, a latex-based ink, can be applied by brush or drawing pen; the image, again on the inside of the screen, is "positive", which means that the first stage consists in blocking out parts of the fabric which will later print.

For this work the artist needs: seroid ink, water-based or cellulose stopping-out medium, a *coating trough*, soapy water, brushes and a very hard rubber.

The actual drawing is carried out as follows: a brush is soaked in soapy water, then dipped in seroid. The artist next paints his picture on the mesh inside the screen as if it were a painter's canvas. In this way the seroid blocks out all that part of the mesh that corresponds to the colour to be printed. Once the drawing or painting in seroid is completed, it is left to dry for about ten minutes, then, the artist, using the coating trough, covers the whole of the interior of the screen, including the image, with a thin, even layer of stopping-out medium; this operation must be carried out in one go.

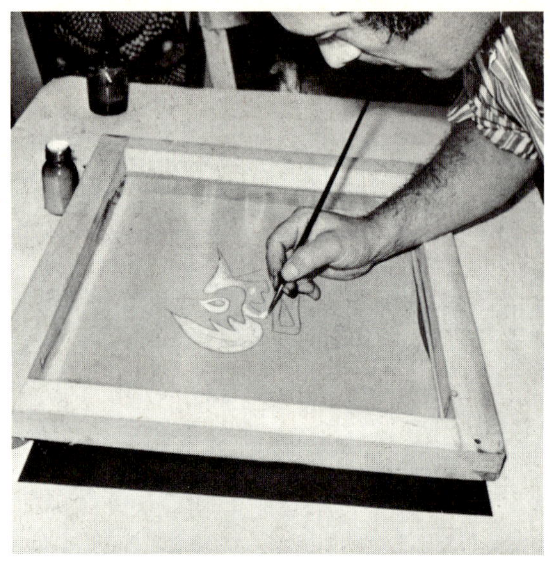

Positive drawing with seroid

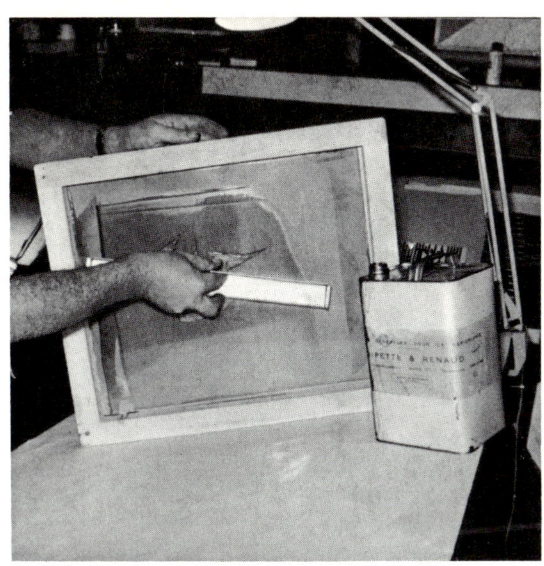

Coating the screen over the seroid (latex) drawing

Removing the seroid with a rubber

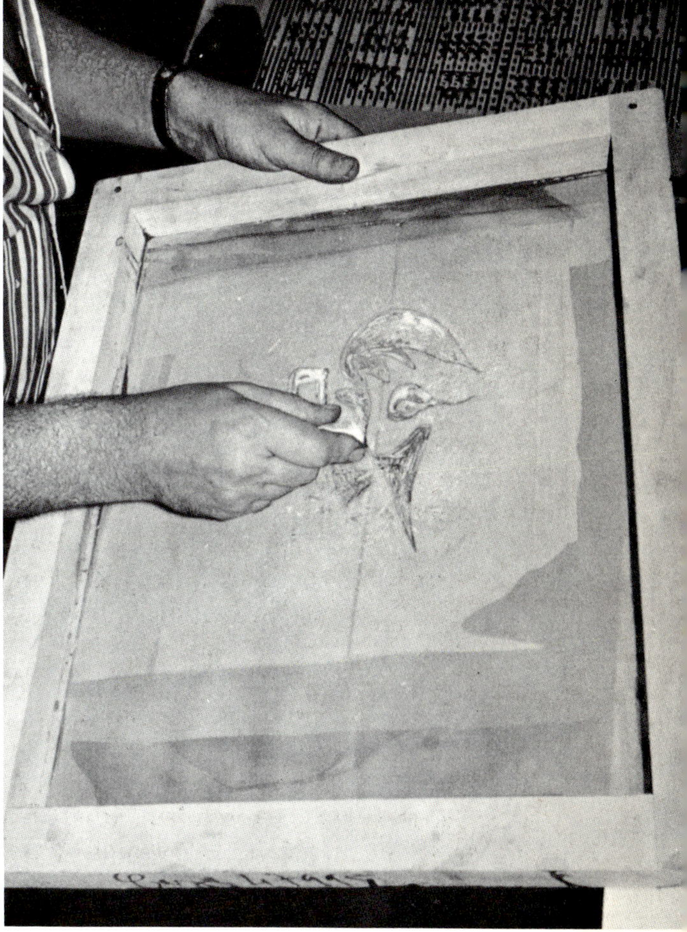

If necessary, a second layer may be applied once the first is completely dry.

When the screen is bone dry, the printing parts of the image are cleared by rubbing with a finger or the eraser. The latex peels off, taking with it the coat of stopping-out medium except for those parts where the medium was in direct contact with the fabric weave, for these are to remain stopped out.

Drawing with litho ink

In principle this technique is similar to the preceding one; litho ink is used instead of seroid, so a solvent is necessary to clean the screen. Some artists prefer this technique because litho ink is easier to use than seroid. As above, once the design has been completed the screen is covered with a layer of stopping-out liquid, but this time it must be water-soluble. When the screen is dry it is turned over and covered with rags impregnated with benzine; after a minute or two the litho ink softens. The screen is then placed upright and rubbed vigorously on both sides, first with rags soaked in benzine, then with dry cloths. This soon eliminates the stopping-out liquid resting on the litho ink, leaving the screen open in the areas destined to print.

Nylogravure

With litho ink or seroid techniques it is very difficult to achieve a fineness of line comparable to burin or dry point work in gravure. The tools for nylogravure are those used in engraving and the technique, although more delicate, is closely related. First, the inside of the screen is coated with a layer of diluted arabic glue, using the coating trough. The coating must be fairly thick and remain inside the screen—which must thus always be dried upside down.

Once dry, the coating of glue is "engraved" with a dry point or burin, care being taken not to damage the mesh itself. For this technique nylon or terylene screens, with between 200 and 300 meshes to the inch, are preferable to fragile silk.

Fernand Léger, Composition, *1950–1951. 5 colour screen print*

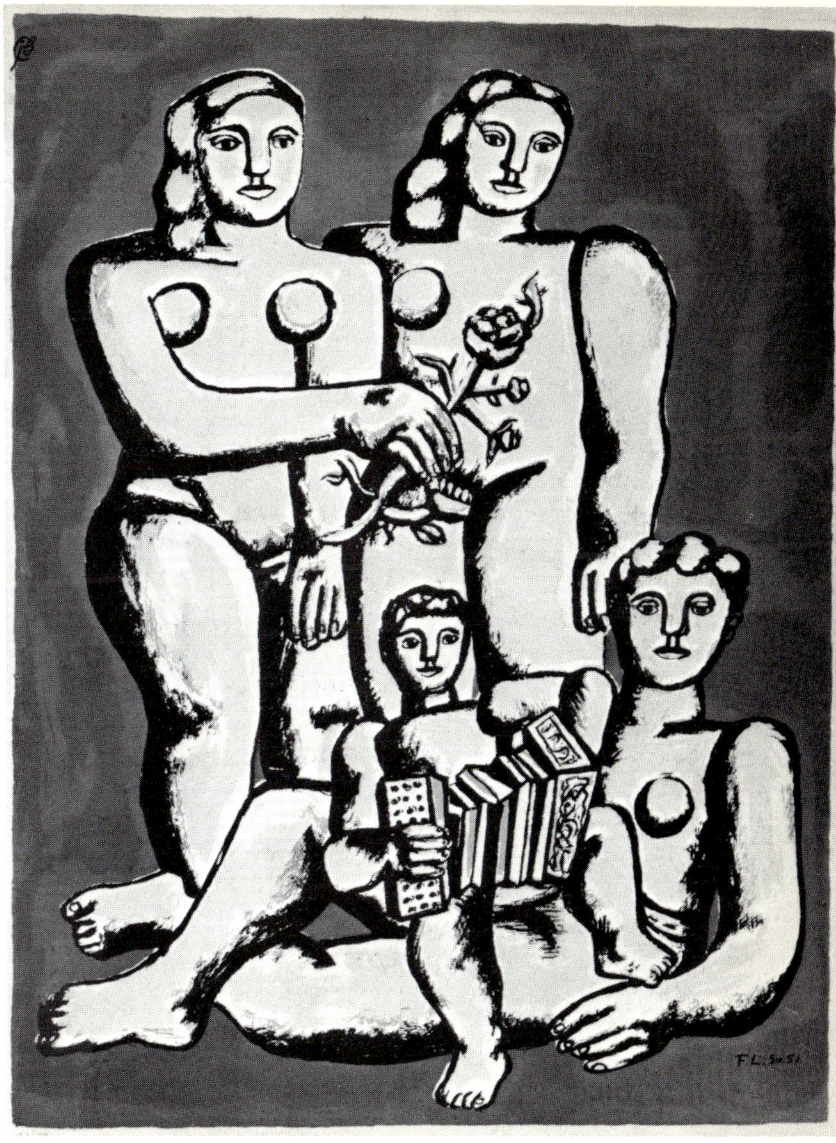
F.L. 50.51

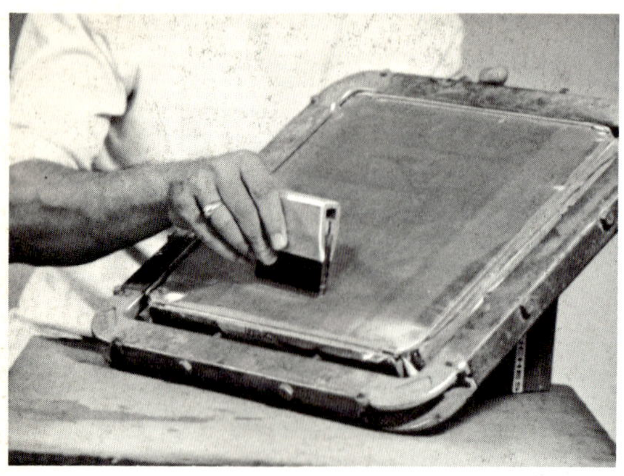

After coating the screen with cellulose varnish, a layer of gelatine is applied to both sides of the frame

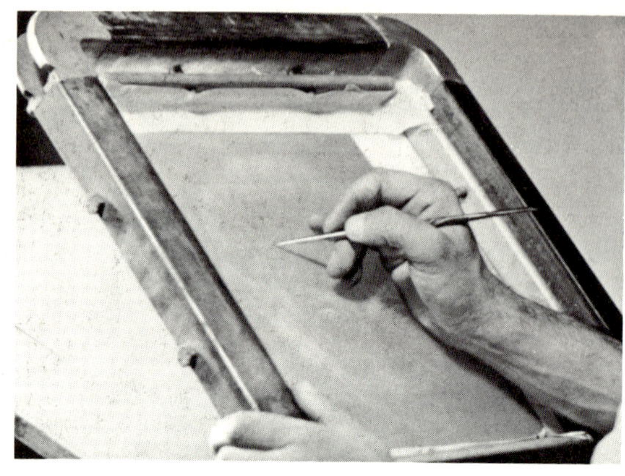

José Mercier engraving with a dry point . . .

The Mercier method

This method, which is called after the Belgian silk screen artist, José Mercier, who perfected it, has great advantages over the preceding technique. It is more accurate and less liable to damage the screen. Here again, a coating trough is used to cover the inside of the screen with a thin layer of cellulose stopping-out liquid. When this is dry a thin coat of liquid wax is applied in the same way, but this time to both sides of the screen. The wax is left to harden and dry; the inside of the screen can then be engraved with a pointed instrument. Only the layer of wax must be removed. When the engraving has been completed, acetone is poured onto the screen; it must cover fully the engraved areas. The artist agitates the screen, then repeats the whole operation with fresh acetone until the stopping-out liquid uncovered by the engraving is completely

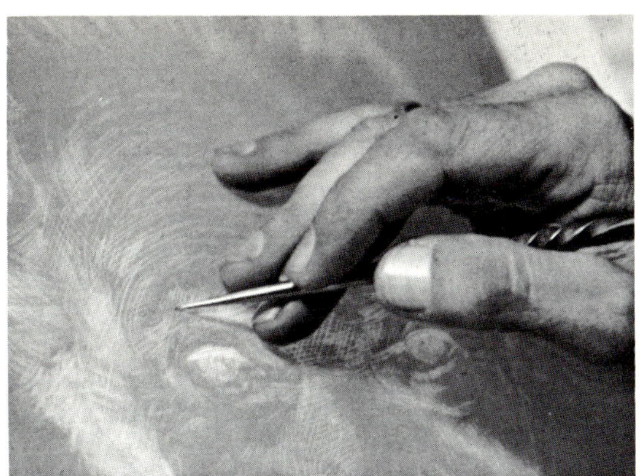

. . . directly on the screen

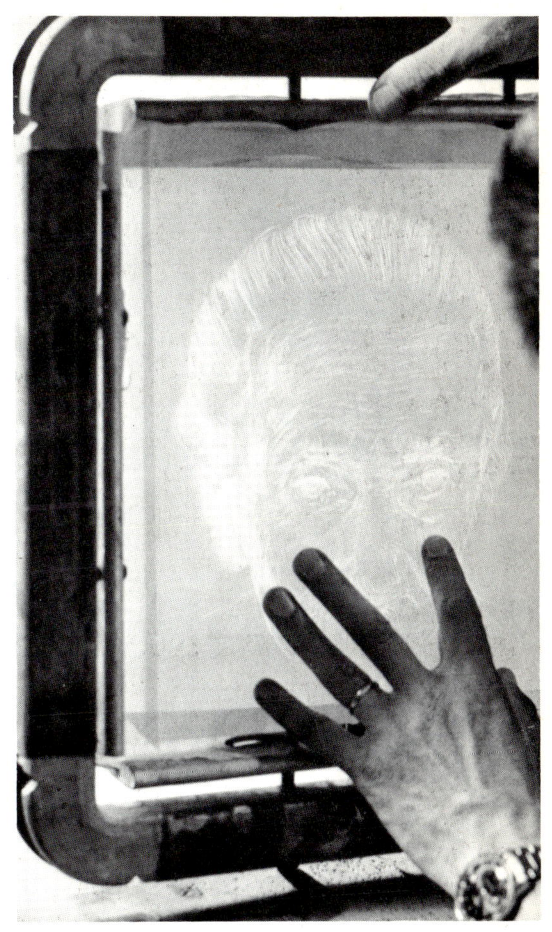

Checking the engraving against the light

dissolved. The acetone is evaporated by a brisk, light rubbing with a dry cloth. The coats of wax are then dissolved with benzine without damaging the stopping-out liquid.

Half-tones

For many artists the ideal forms of graphic expression are not necessarily flat colour or line. It was long believed that although silk screen offered great possibilities for

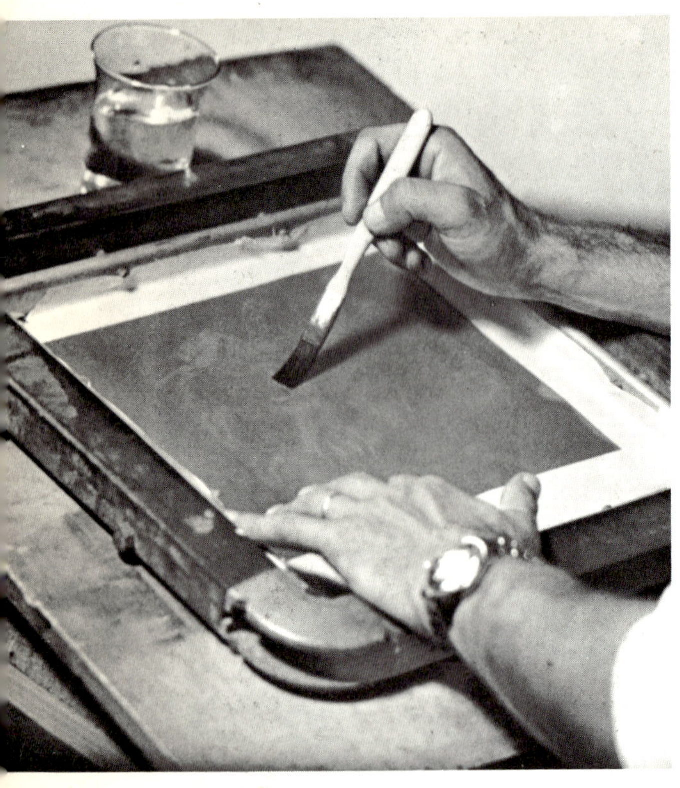

The screen is cleared with acetone

working with flat colours, it was unsuitable for half-tones. American artists, who were the first to use silk screen, found a way around this difficulty by using a number of screens for the same colour, darkening and blocking off more of the colour on each screen in succession: This resulted in some interesting prints, but could mean printing up to 90 times on the same sheet of paper! But in fact it is possible to achieve as many subtleties and half-tones with silk screen as in lithography. While it is perhaps preferable, for this purpose, to use various stencil papers which are worked on away from the screen itself and then transferred photochemically, there is one technique which permits direct work on the screen: litho crayon.

Litho crayon

Even though it is possible to use Terylene and nylon for this technique, the rougher texture of silk gives better results. A taffeta weave silk with 170 meshes to the inch renders the initial design excellently. For silk screen the most suitable lithographic crayons are numbers 1, 2 and 3. The artist can either create freely on the screen or follow an original sketch placed as a guide a fraction of an inch under the screen. The more pressure exerted in drawing, the more the mesh is blocked and the darker the effect on printing; it must be remembered that only mesh completely blocked by the crayon will let ink pass through after development. The screen can be checked against the light from time to time, but it is always advisable to work darker than the colours desired on the print as the discontinuity of the mesh results in an image which is slightly less dense than the drawing on the silk.

Very interesting effects can be obtained by placing the screen directly onto a textured surface like emery paper, glass paper, wire mesh, rough wood, etc.; the crayon will only fill the mesh of the screen where it touches the asperities of the textured support.

Positive drawing with litho crayon

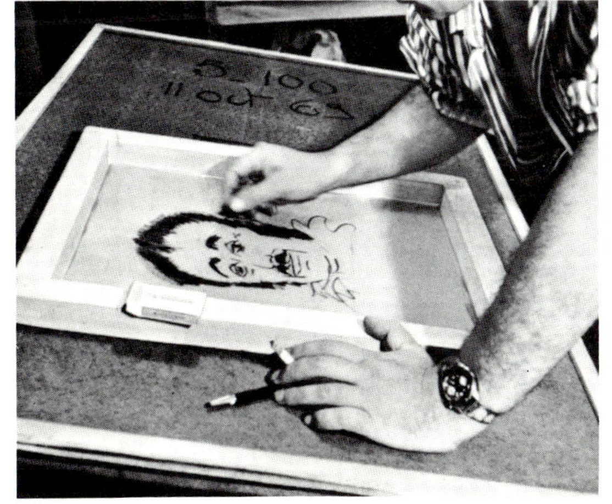

Coating the screen over the litho crayon drawing

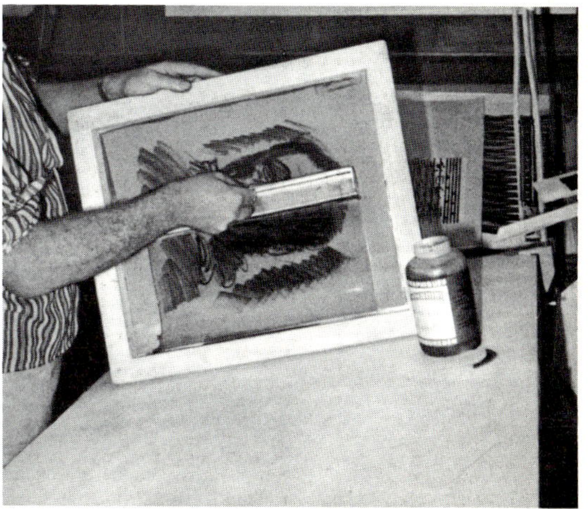

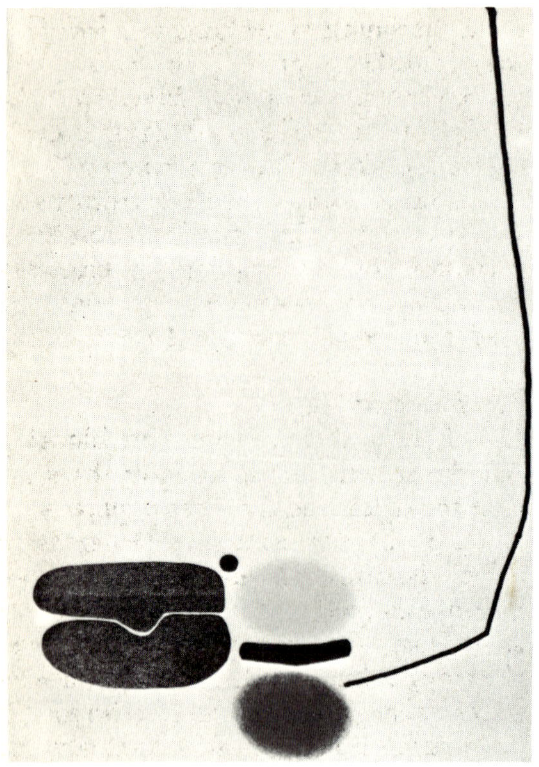

Victor Pasmore, Variation *4, 1972. Colour screen print*

Once the drawing is completed, as for the litho ink technique, a thin coat of stopping-out liquid is pushed across the inside of the screen, over the drawing, with a coating trough.

The screen is dried, turned over and rested on rags soaked in benzine. After twenty minutes the crayon drawing has softened and dissolved: by rubbing both sides of the screen simultaneously with a dry cloth the stopping-out liquid which is not in direct contact with the screen, but only adhering to the crayon drawing, is eliminated. Any remaining traces of litho crayon or obstructed mesh must be cleaned out by rubbing both sides of the screen again with rags soaked in fresh benzine.

Simultaneous effects of flat colour, line and shading can of course be obtained by combining the techniques of seroid, litho ink and lithographic crayon on the same screen.

4 WORKING INDIRECTLY AWAY FROM THE SCREEN

Purely technical obligations or limitations may impede or prevent the artist from expressing himself freely directly on the mesh. He can and should, then, without detracting from the originality of his work, create away from the screen itself. One technique which produces results of extraordinary accuracy and precision—hand-cut stencils—can in fact only be carried out away from the screen.

Hand-cut stencil papers

Of all the techniques used for blocking out the screen, stencilling is at the same time the oldest and the most popular with amateurs of flat colour. The hand-cut stencil is really the ancestor of all silk screen techniques. At first, as in simple stencilling, knife-cut paper, thin metal sheeting, celluloid, gelatine and varnished papers were all used. The first "modern" hand-cut stencils were films consisting of three layers: the film itself, a coat of adhesive and a sheet of transparent paper. The top layer, the film of shellac setting liquid, was cut with a razor-sharp scalpel in those parts of the image intended to print then pealed off and disposed with;

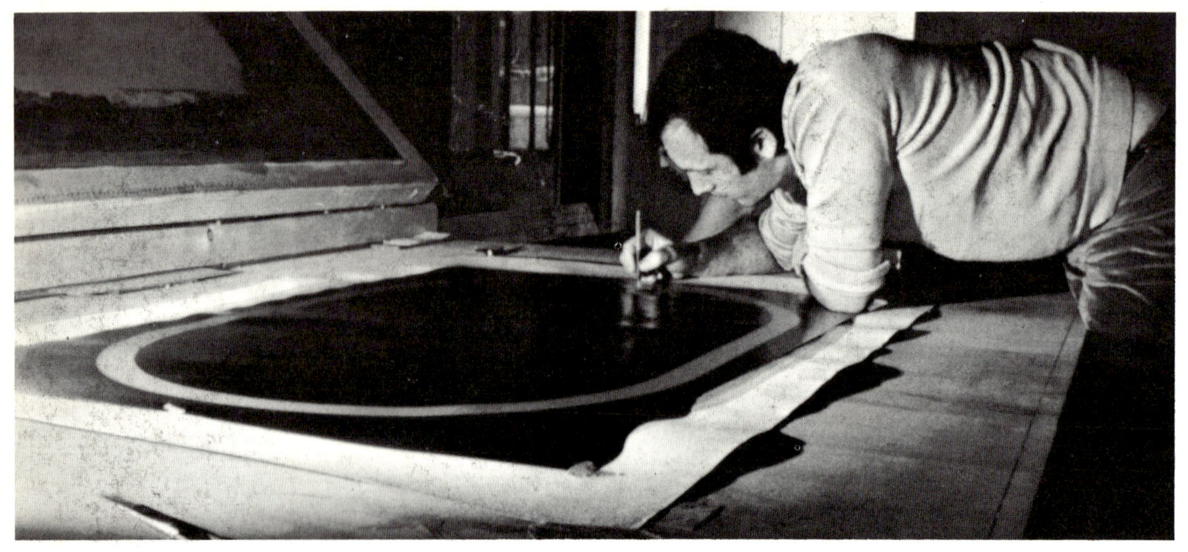

Cutting a stencil by hand with a scalpel

the remaining areas, corresponding to the parts of the screen to be stopped-out, remained attached to the transparent paper-backing by the intermediary layer of adhesive. The film was then placed under a clean silk screen, in close contact with it, and the silk ironed with a warm iron; this caused the top coating of the film to adhere to the fabric. All that remained to be done was to peel off the transparent backing which had acted as a temporary support for the film during cutting.

These films, being applied with a hot iron, could not be used on synthetic fabric and were also fairly difficult to cut; they have been gradually replaced by more elaborate films in which the surface fusion

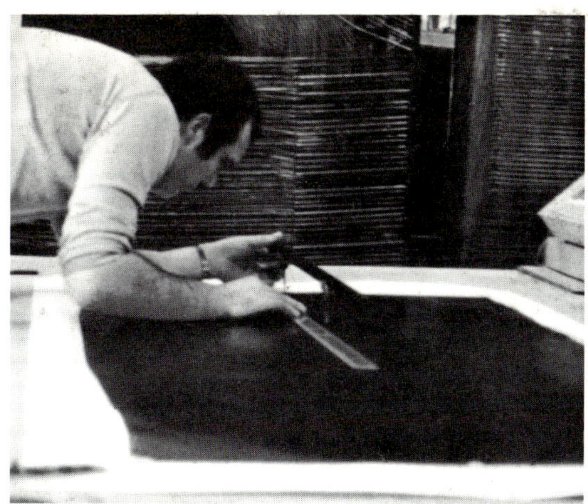

Cutting by hand

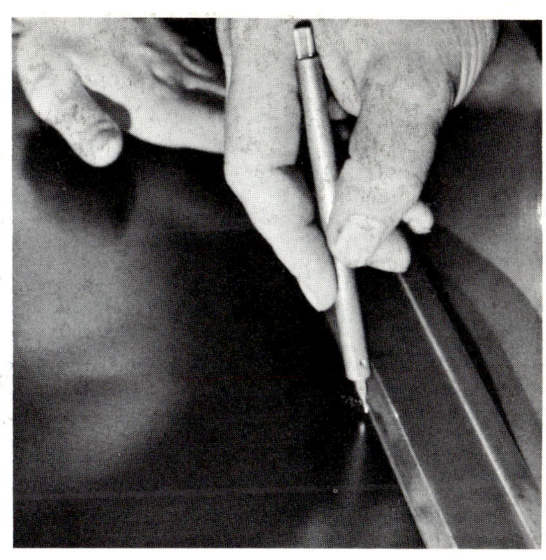

causing adherence to the screen is achieved either by means of a specific solvent or by water. The modern films are either cellulose (these are the most popular) or water-based. They have a disposable backing of either transparent paper or plastic (the latter are slightly more stable, but also more expensive). The cellulose films can be used with all inks soluble in white spirit (or other mineral solvents); the water-based variety are used with all inks requiring plastic solvents (cellulose, vinyl, acrylic). An artist can, of course, cut directly into a film, but he generally makes a precise sketch of his work on paper first. He then fixes over it a film of slightly larger dimensions: his sketch is clearly visible through the transparent

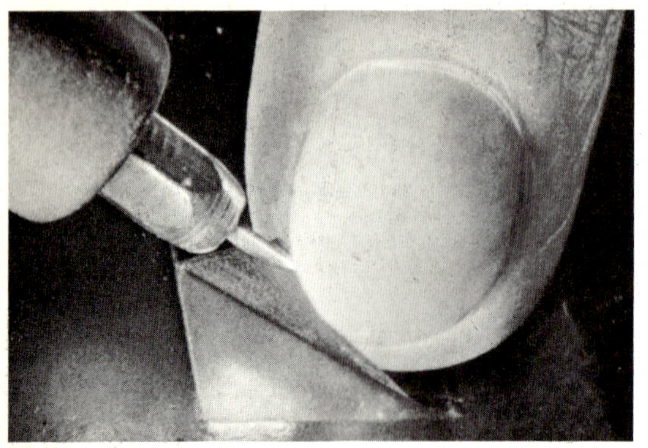

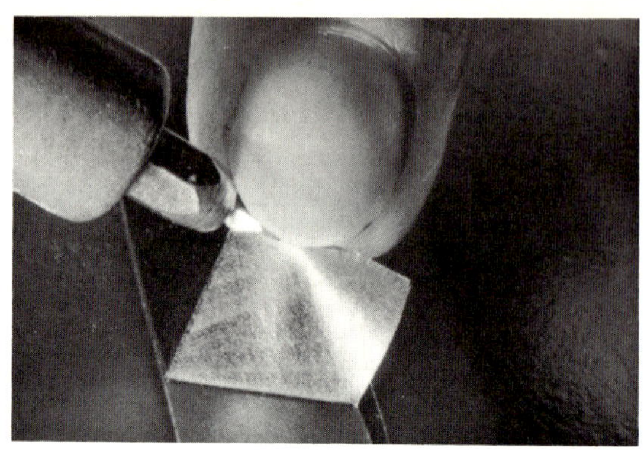

film. The cutting itself is carried out with a scalpel which must be extremely sharp. It can be done free-hand, or with the help of rulers, compasses and French curves. The fineness of the design and shapes depends on the artist's ability alone. This technique indeed demands a touch both sure and light: sure, to exclude trembling, ragged curves; and light, because it is of the utmost importance to slice no deeper than the superficial coating of the film: if excess pressure causes the provisional backing paper layer to be touched by the blade, there is a risk of damage to the edges of the stencil during adhesion to the screen by an accumulation

Stripping a hand-cut stencil

of solvent in the cut. Powerful and slightly oblique lighting is of great help when cutting stencil film, as it shows up the incision traced by the scalpel. Once the stencil has been cut the unwanted parts of film are peeled off, still using a scalpel.

The stencil thus cut and stripped of part of its film is placed under the screen, in direct contact with the fabric. The artist then prepares two pieces of wadding, one soaked in a solvent suitable for the film being used (this is always either supplied or indicated by the manufacturer), the other large and dry. The film is then impregnated through the fabric, a small area at a time, and immediately rubbed briskly, but without applying pressure, with the dry wadding. The whole surface of the stencil is treated in this manner; a change in colour marks those areas that adhere to the screen.

After two or three minutes, in the case of a cellulose film, or twenty minutes if it is a water-based film, the provisional backing can be removed. All that remains to be done is to block out the screen all round the film with a filler liquid of

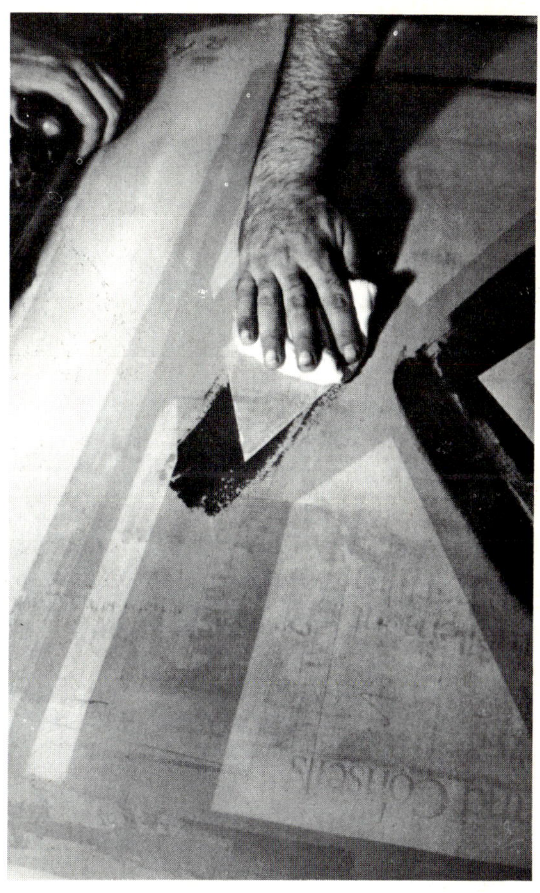

Sticking the stencil to the bottom of the screen

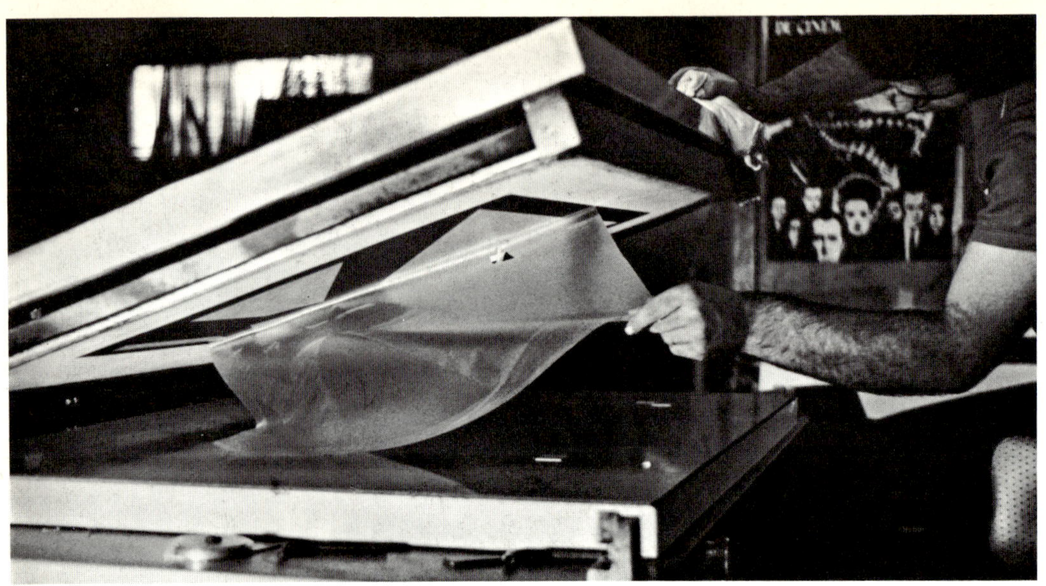

Peeling off the temporary backing once the stencil has adhered to the screen

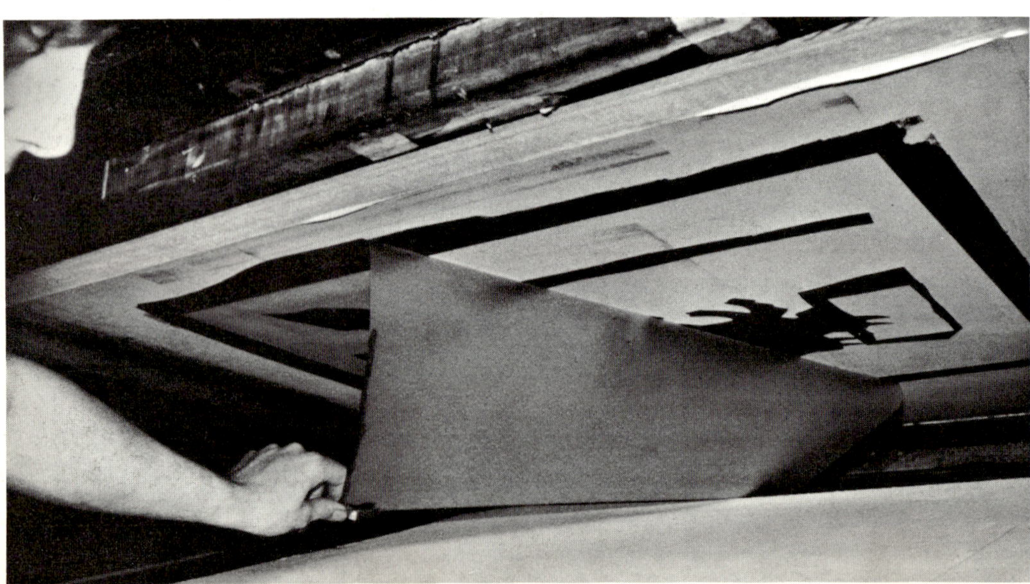

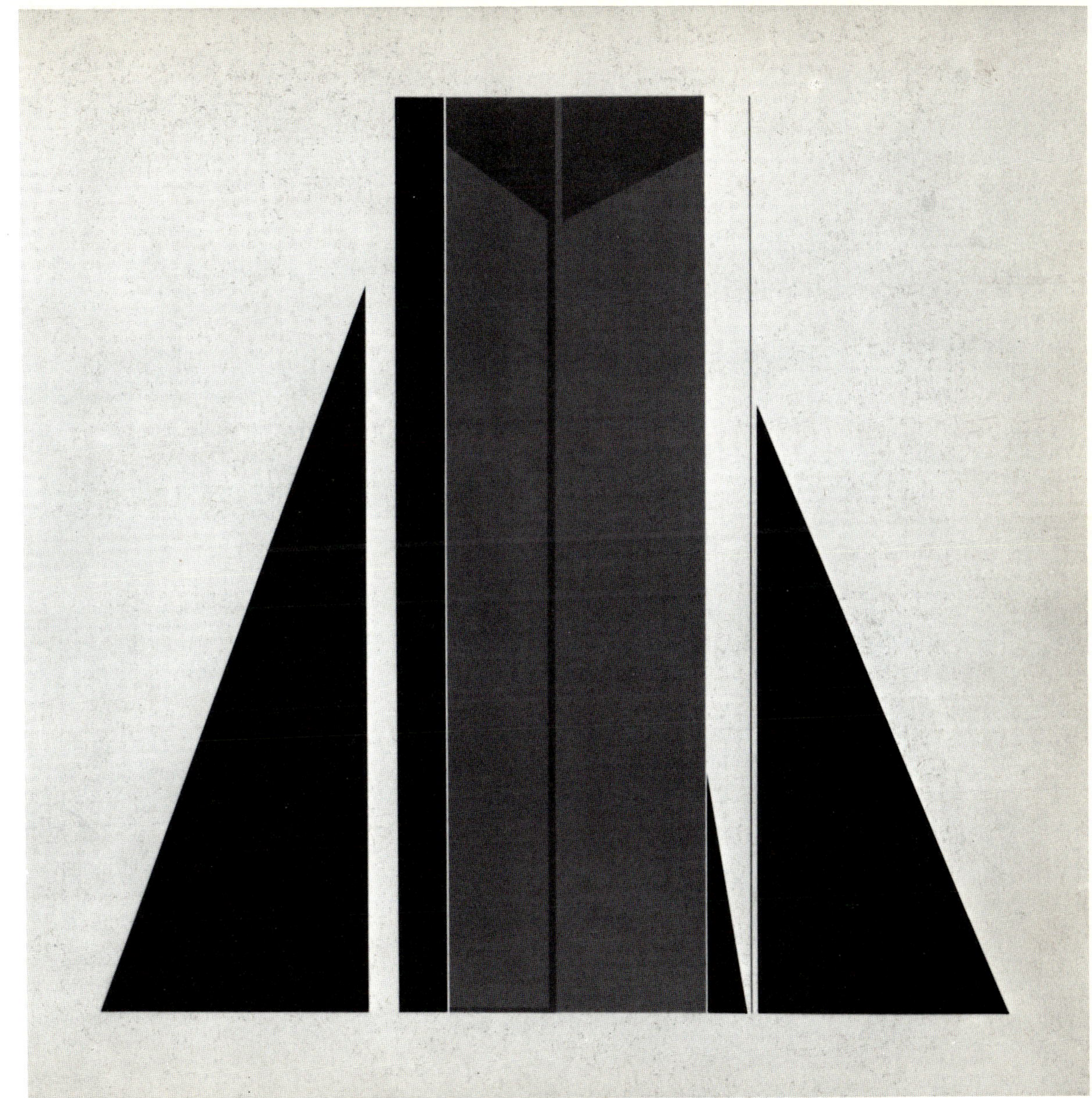

similar composition. After printing, the film can be removed with acetone or warm water, depending on its chemical composition.

Photochemical techniques

As we have seen, in many cases the artist's liberty of expression is limited, especially as far as half-tones and shading are concerned, by techniques which involve working directly on the screen and even by the hand-cut stencils method. This has led serigraphers to turn increasingly to photochemical techniques where the artist carries out his design on an intermediary support, a *transparent positive*, or *diapositive*, from which it is transferred onto or under the screen photochemically.

Most of these techniques are based on the properties of colloids such as gelatine, P.V.A., polyamides and polyethylenes—which on being sensitized to light by the application, usually, of ammonium or potassium bichromate—harden and become relatively insoluble in water when exposed to very actinic light (rich in ultra-violet rays).

Very roughly, these techniques can be divided into three main groups:

- Direct stencilling; the whole screen is coated with a light-sensitive emulsion then dried, exposed and developed;
- indirect stencilling; a sensitized gelatine film is exposed, developed, then placed under the screen; the softened gelatine sticks in the mesh while drying;
- direct-indirect stencilling; a combination of the first two methods.

In each case the transparent positive is in close contact with the screen or film; it is placed between them and the light source. The "positive" areas, which are usually black or red, prevent the light from hardening the whole of the film or emulsion; areas not exposed to the light stay soluble and disappear when the film is developed in water, thus permitting the passage of ink during printing.

Obviously these techniques call for slightly more complicated and elaborate material than the manual methods described above. Without going to the

◁ *Jean Baier,* Composition, *1971. 4 colour screen print*

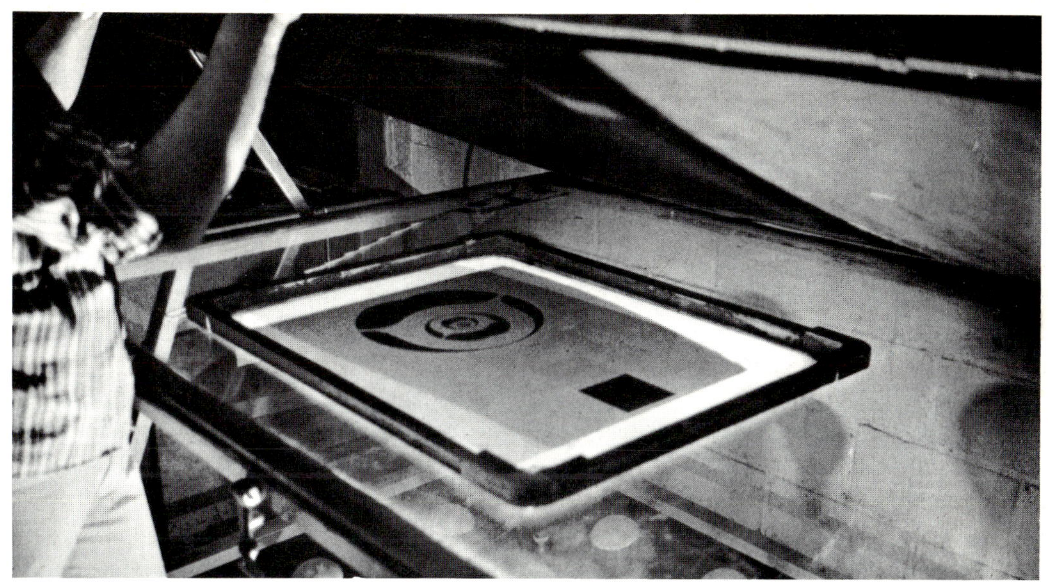

The screen is placed in a pneumatic exposure chassis

length of setting up a complete laboratory, certain minimum requirements must nevertheless be met; to wit: running hot and cold water with a mixer and a shower head, an area where screens coated with sensitized emulsion can dry away from the light, ventilation and, of course, material for exposure: a source of actinic light (MBR/U mercury vapour lamps are the simplest and the most practical) and a contact box.

A full, detailed description of the techniques, emulsions and various films used for photographic stencil making is inevitably outside the scope of this book. However, manufacturers always supply

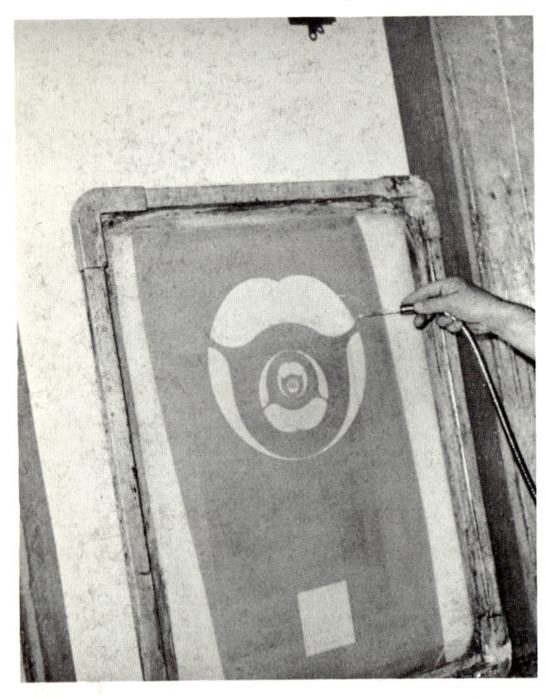

The direct screen stencil is developed by a jet of cold water

the necessary instructions on the use of their products. Emulsions and films are available either presensitized or requiring sensitizing when ready for use. They can be handled and coated with emulsion in subdued artificial light, but never by daylight.

Which methods and fabrics should the artist choose?

In the past, the major drawback of the direct method, simpler and less expensive, was that it was impossible to reproduce on a fabric with rather open mesh a line free from a sort of saw-tooth effect; this being caused, on developing the screen, by a swelling of the emulsion in the apertures of the mesh. Since the film used for the indirect method is developed away from the screen it does not swell and can thus, when later fixed under the screen, "cut across" the mesh. There now exist more elaborate emulsions which limit the swelling; and also the extremely fine modern synthetic fabrics render the saw-tooth effect invisible to the naked eye. For both methods it is wise to choose synthetic screens of terylene or nylon, as the concentrated potassium chloride bleach used to clean the screen after printing damages silk irretrievably. For the reasons discussed above, if the direct method is chosen, fine screens with between 300 and 450 meshes to the inch should be used. For indirect stencilling, practically any quality from about 110 meshes to the inch upwards is suitable; it is chosen in function of the thickness of ink desired and the fineness of the subject.

Making the transparent positive

The transparent positive is an indispensable intermediary in fixing a stencil on a screen photochemically. It can be made in many ways, by hand or photographically. Nowadays photography as a basis for artistic expression can no longer be ignored, nor can it be denied that a great many artists have discovered in it a perfectly "original" means of expression, so long as they do not limit themselves to mere reproduction. In fact, quite a few young artists possess extremely sophisticated photographic laboratories where they carry out their creative search for new effects, experimenting with solarisation, line-photo, equidensities, isodensities,

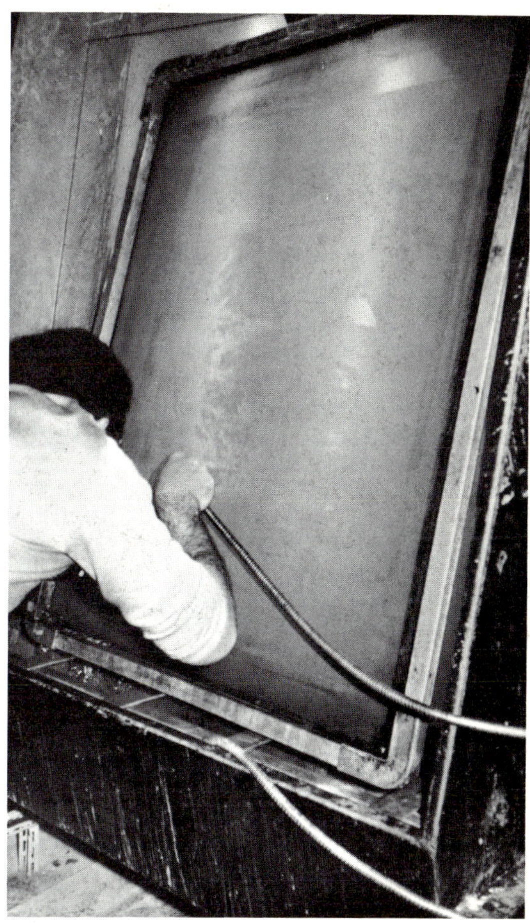

Indirect stencilling: developed with hot water

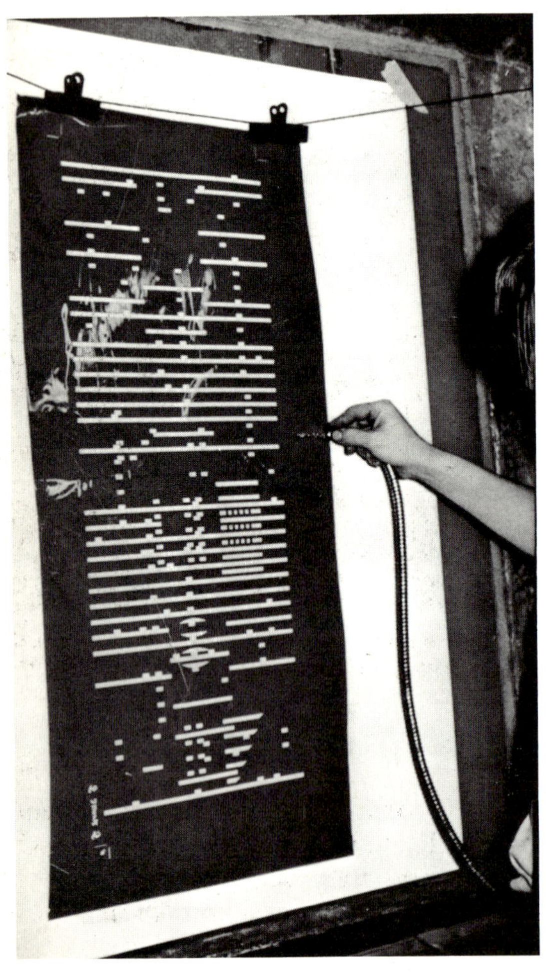

stage-by-stage printing and even screen dot work and other such novelties. The powerful alliance of imagination and technique in this field has resulted in a great flurry of creative artistic activity. The least one can say about it is that it is not lacking in "originality".

Hand-made transparent positives

Here we meet again nearly all the techniques used in the direct method. Working away from the screen simply offers the double advantage of easier execution and a wider field of expression. The principle, however, remains the same: the parts of a transparent or translucent sheet of plastic which correspond to the areas of the image intended to print must be rendered opaque to actinic light. Now, black is not the only colour to be opaque to blue actinic light; the films and emulsions manufactured for photochemical screen stencils are in fact orthochromatic and not panchromatic, so that reds, browns, dark violet, and amber all block out light as effectively as opaque black.

The film is developed

Brush work

Although it is perfectly possible to work on transparent surfaces like acetate, it is worth using specialized supports such as the dulled acetate Kodatrace or Astrafoil. The brush or pen drawing is done with brown retouching gouache, India ink or plastic inks; they must all simply be opaque to actinic light. As many transparent positives are made as there are colours to be printed, either by tracing over a sketch placed under the positive or free-hand.

Retouching is done with a scraper, and the opacity is finally checked against a light-screen.

Hand-cut transparent positives

Here we find again the advantages of hand-cut stencils: absolutely clean edges, no large areas to be blocked out with gouache, great speed of execution, with the additional possibility of brush-work effects on the developed areas of the film. Special red or amber films (rubylith or amberlith) are used; they are composed of a cellulose coating attached to a transparent support by a light adhesive. Cutting is done with a scalpel, the only difference being that this is a positive technique: the film is left on its backing in those parts of the design which are meant to print, and peeled off around them.

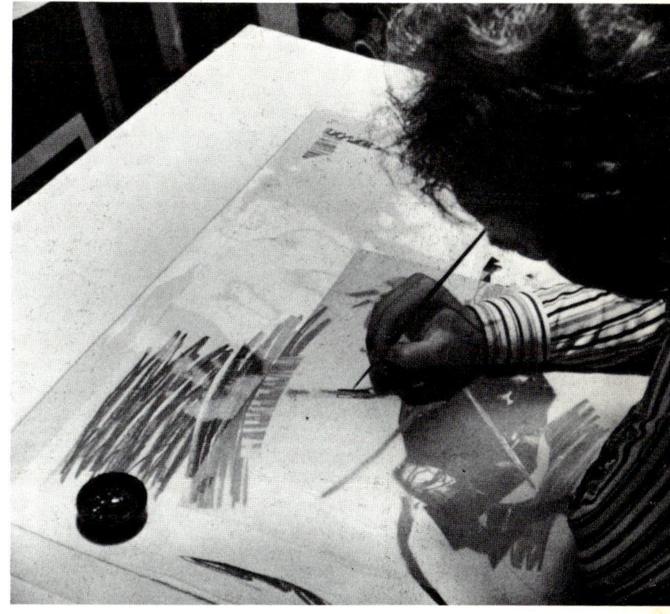

To make a transparent positive the screen-printer works with opaque gouache on "Kodatrace" transparent film

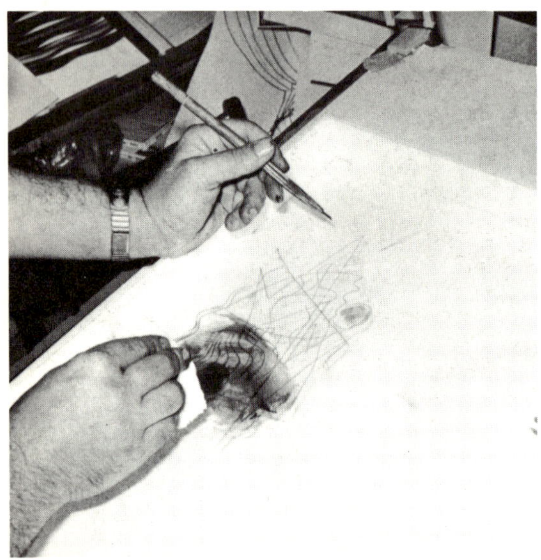

Engraving with a dry point on transparent plastic, the engraved design is filled with opaque ink

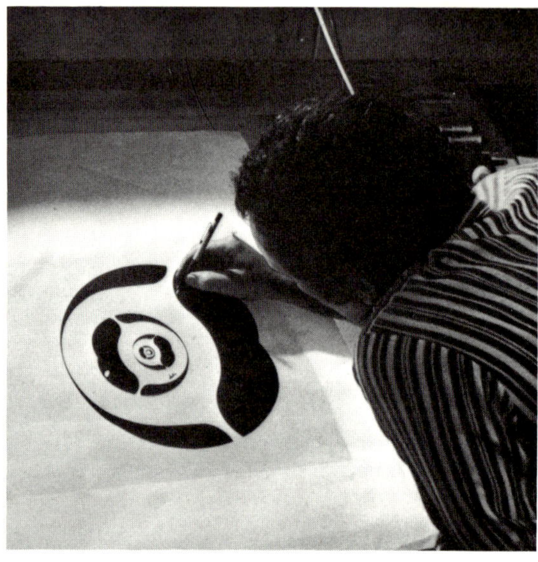

"Rubylith" film hand-cut transparent positive stencil

Engraved transparent positives

Some effects cannot be obtained with the above techniques: crisp penstrokes, scraping-out, graining, etc. These limitations can be overcome by using a plate of transparent metachrylate (Perspex) about 1/24″ thick on which the artist engraves the design and the effects he wishes to transfer to the screen, using a dry-point, burin, scraper, cutting-knife and glass paper. When the engraving has been completed, he covers the whole surface with opaque ink, using a pad of wadding. He then wipes the surface of the plate with a soft cloth; the ink remains only in the engraved design. This operation can be repeated several times until the hollow image is perfectly filled.

Working with lithographic crayon

All the preceding techniques are classically "silk screen": perfect for line and flat colour work, but unsuitable for shading and half-tones. All degrees of these can, however, be obtained by silk screen techniques, including effects which at first sight would be considered as purely lithographic. The material used is either an acetate dulled by sand-blasting or a special support called Diracop which is sold in different grains varying in fineness and aspect. Working with various qualities of lithographic crayon, an artist can obtain effects quite similar to those of lithography.

Photographic transparent positives

The know-how and equipment required to produce a transparent positive photographically constitute too vast a subject for it to be treated here. All the effects described above can be achieved photographically. One thing is essential, however: the film must always be of the very high-contrast "lith" type. The transparent positive, by definition, is never a

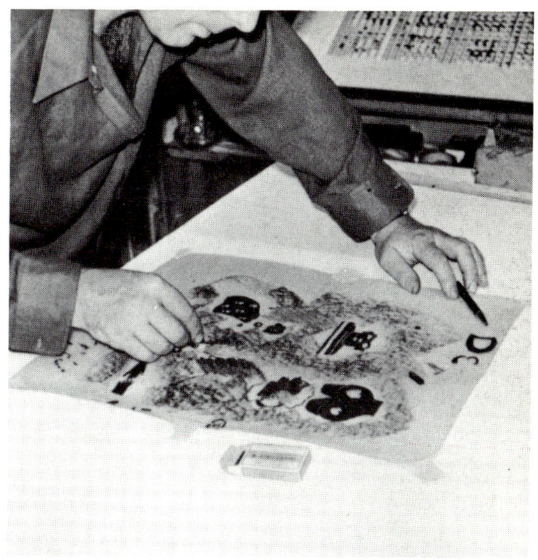

Working with litho crayon and gouache on "grained" transparent plastic

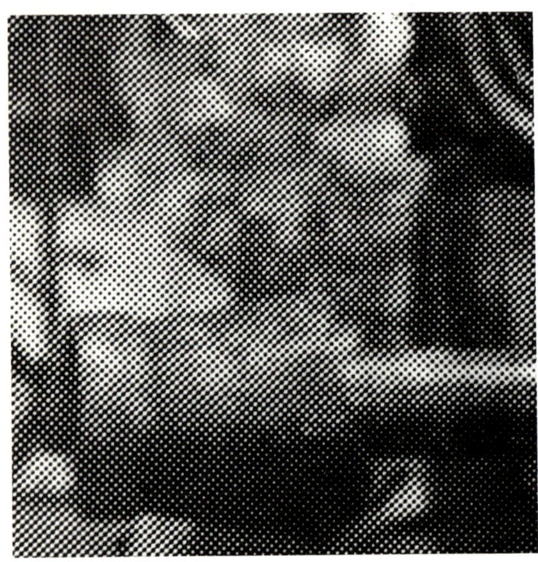

Enlarged photomechanical screen dots used in a print by Gérard Fromanger (detail)

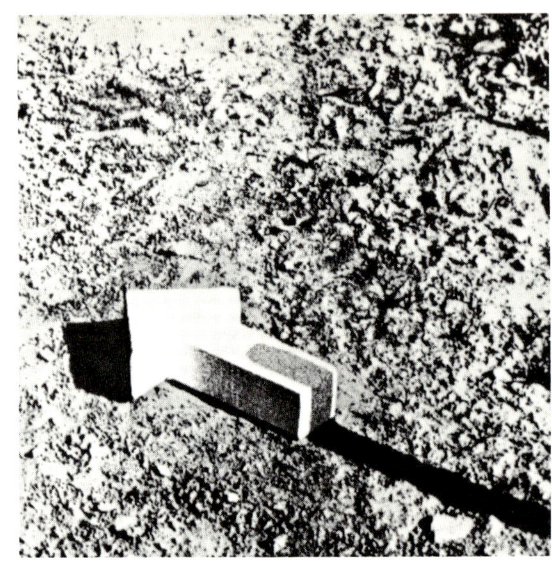

Gianfredo Camesi, Mouvement 1971, *1972. Black and white screen print (detail)*

"negative", and the sensitive coating of the film must always be the "right way round" with respect to the image.

And what about the half-tone screen? Should it be used or not? Normally, this photographic device is used to translate a half-tone negative into dots of varying diameter which give the impression of nuances and shading. As a means of reproduction it should be avoided in

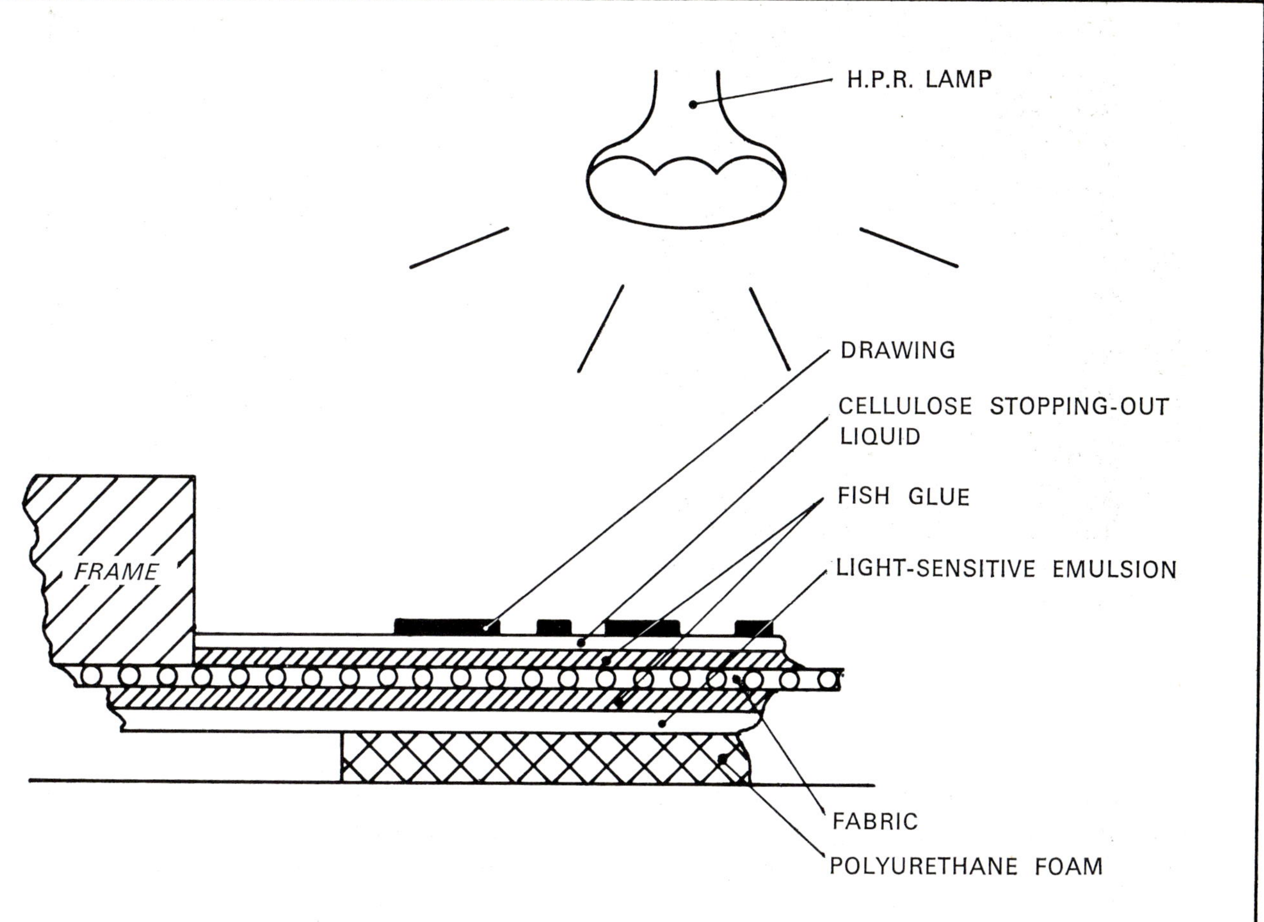

Order of coatings for the Linstead method

serigraphy. But it is altogether quite a different matter if, as is done by certain artists, it is used as a graphic image in its own right, in the form of magnified screen dots, for instance, or of linear or circular screen effects, or again of greatly enlarged photographs with a coarse "newspaper" grain. Then its use is warranted, for it plays an essential role in the composition of an original work.

Several of the various techniques we have been discussing can, of course, be mixed on a single transparent positive, just as several positives can be superimposed. All depends on the effect sought. There exist self-adhesive half-tone screens, signs and letters that can be added to the positive. Or one can glue on pieces of torn paper, blackened lace, fabrics, etc. or again one can use a spray-gun, a pressurized inkspray can or an air-brush.

The Linstead mixed method

This technique, which is called after the American painter Linstead, combines photochemical treatment of the screen with direct work. A screen of terylene or nylon with between 230 and 360 meshes to the inch is first sized back and front with a thin layer of transparent fish glue; when dry, the inside of the screen only is given a thin coating of colourless cellulose stopping-out liquid. This coating receives the design in opaque gouache or India ink. Self-adhesive dot-screen and letters can be added; they must also be opaque. Once the design is completed, the outside of the screen is covered with a layer of direct photo stencil emulsion. This is left to dry away from the light, then the inside of the screen is exposed to a mercury vapour lamp for about fifteen minutes. It is developed by spraying a jet of warm water over the outside of the screen: the emulsion, which has been protected from the light by the opaque parts of the design, is washed away, taking with it the superimposed layers of size and cellulose stopping-out liquid, and, of course, the opaque gouache.

Victor Vasarely, Composition, *1966. Colour screen print*

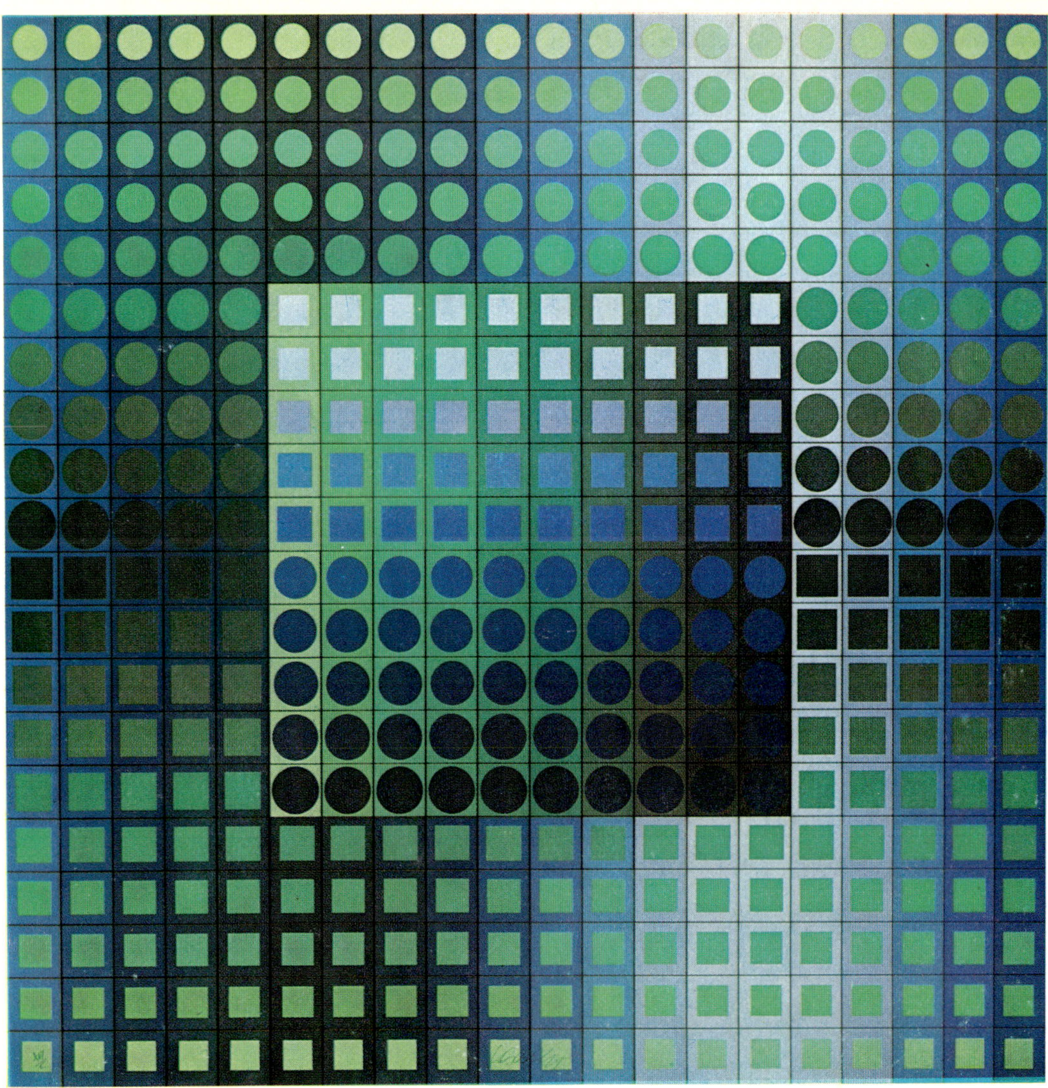

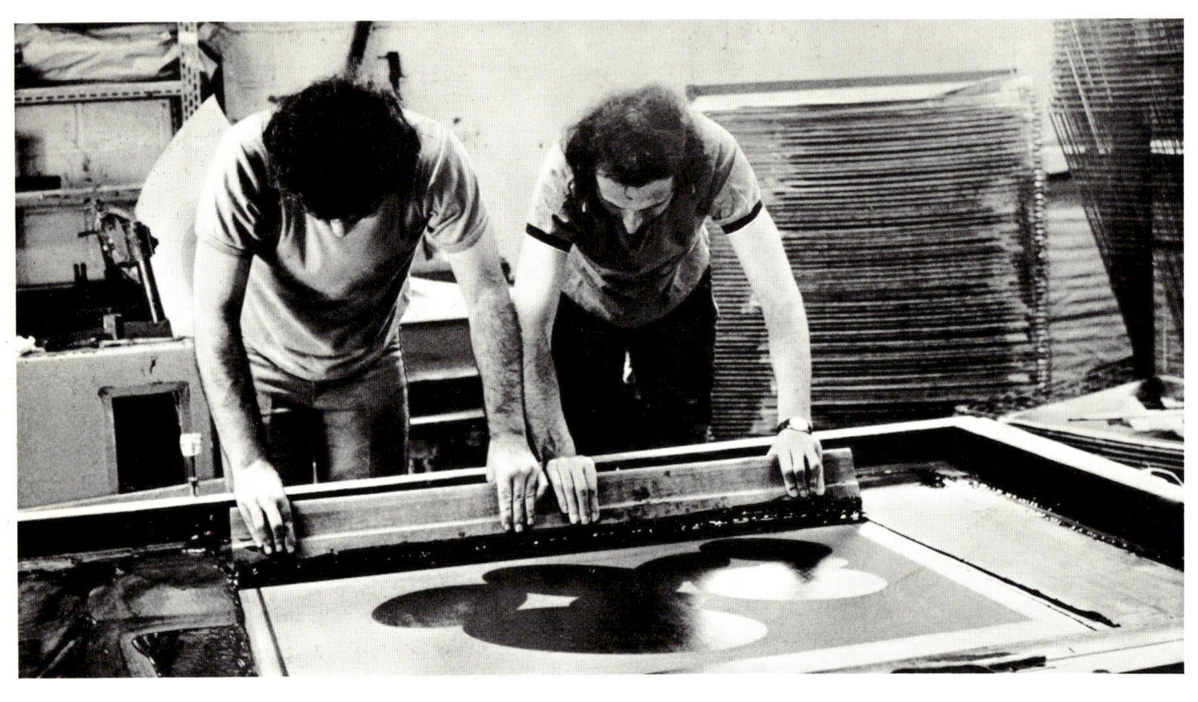

Pulling a giant print with the artist's help

5 PRINTING

Like a lithograph an original print screen is always, by definition, printed by hand, or at least partly by hand. A hand press is a press in which the registration of the sheet of paper and inking with the squeegee are done entirely by hand. Using a semi-manual press the sheet of paper is placed in its guides by hand, but the movement of the squeegee and screen lifting are mechanical. Automatic or semi-automatic presses in which the whole process, including the registration of the paper, is carried out automatically, are not suitable for art silk screen and should therefore be proscribed.

What to print on?

One of the principal characteristics of silk screen is that any surface can be printed on.

Paper

Paper is the traditional material for printing, particularly high-quality rag paper such as Arches, Lana and Japan. These papers usually have one "good" corner, cut to a perfect right-angle; this is placed against the registration-guides (silk screen registration is never done with needles).

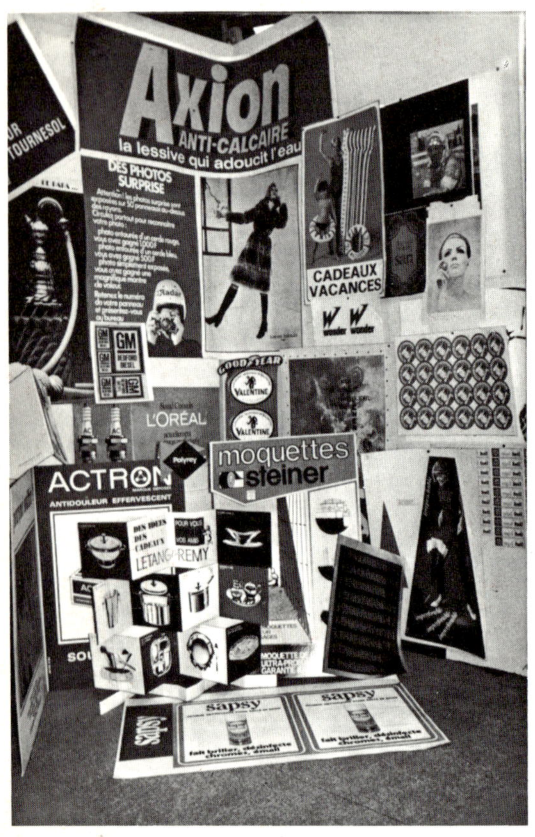

Backings which can be used for printing

Superimposition of transparent inks in screen printing: 63 different tints are obtained from 6 printing colours ▷ (p. 61)

Many artists are content with Bristol-board, heavy offset paper, water-colour paper, cartridge paper, etc. Other artists also use ultra-brilliant plastified papers like Chromolux and Kromecote. These often call for special inks, more mordant than those generally chosen for paper. It should be noted, however, that screen printing is less dependent on the choice of paper than lithography because of the thickness of the ink layer that can be printed.

Other materials

Current artistic research in the graphic arts tends to focus on other materials than paper. Screen printing alone can make this sort of experimentation possible, thanks to the diversity of the chemical composition of the inks available and the mechanical suppleness of the mesh stretched on the screen.

The other materials which can be printed on include cardboard, matt or gloss metallized paper, aluminium (either polished or anodized), plain or painted sheet metal, fabrics laminated (or not) to paper, leather, wood, glass, and numerous

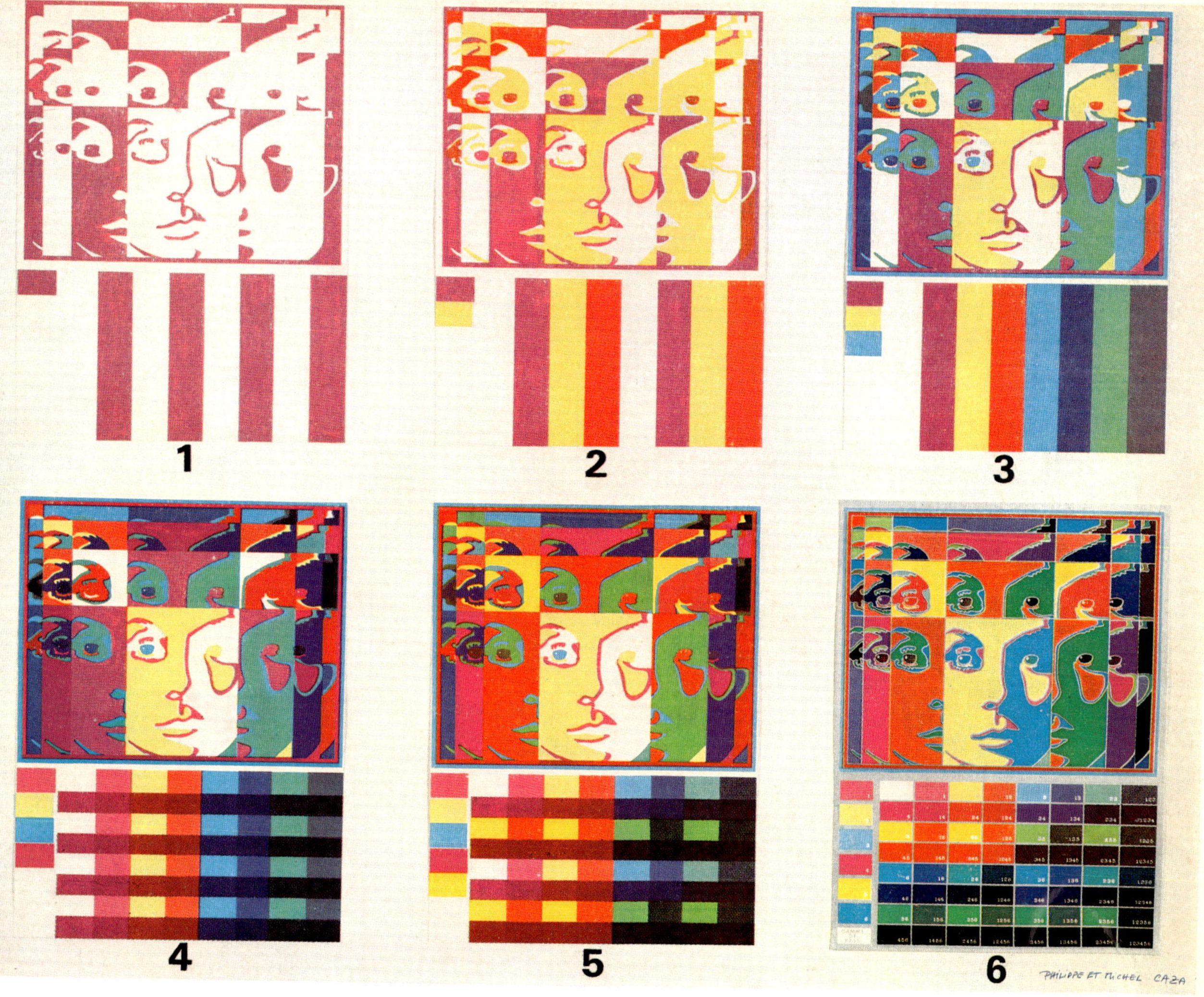
1
2
3
4
5
6
PHILIPPE ET MICHEL CAZA

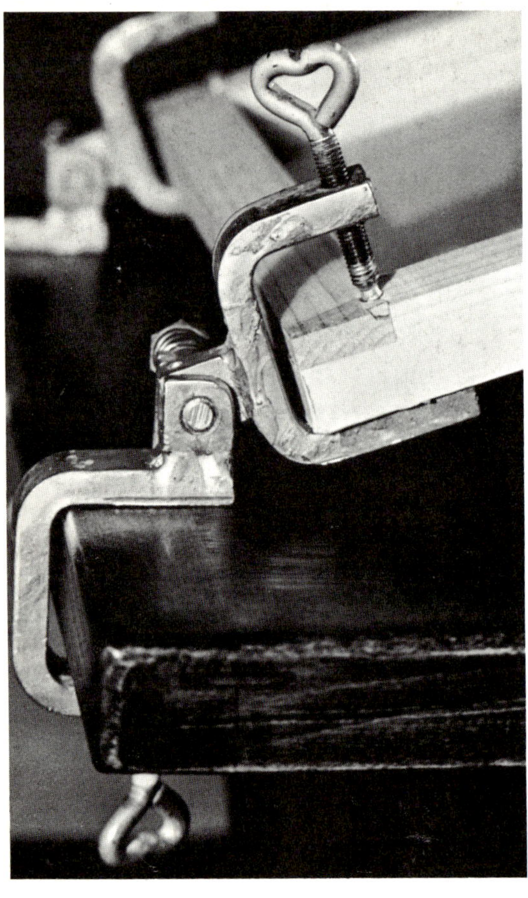

Typical hand-printing hinges

ing results can be obtained, if, in geometric progression, all possible combinations of a few superimposed colours are used. Let us take three colours: A, B, C; with them we can obtain 7 different tints: A, B, A + B, C, A + C, B + C, A + B + C; every new colour added to and combined with each of the previous colours and combinations of these, doubles the total number of colours plus one—the new one. It is easy to imagine the rich harvest that can be reaped from this system by an artist and screen printer with a talent for colour working together on a print. A word of warning, however—this technique calls for great skill and perfect registration if a "blurred" effect is to be avoided. Also, colour-guide proofs must be run off on the press beforehand enabling the artist to tell at a glance the tints he will be able to obtain during printing.

The printing table

One can, if necessary, make do with a screen attached by two hinges to a level table to create valid works of art—in fact many artists have done so. There are certainly hundreds of hand presses or semi-manual presses especially designed for screen printing; costly, mechanically more complex versions, are professional screen printer's equipment, but the materials necessary for setting up a handpress oneself are perfectly easy to acquire and assemble.

Let us recapitulate the principles of silk screen printing: the frame is attached to a flat base by a more or less intricate hinge system. The sheet of paper destined to receive the printed image is aligned against the registration guides. The screen is then lowered, by hand or mechanically, into position, that is to say parallel to the paper but not quite touching it (between $^1/_4$ and $^1/_{24}$ of an inch away); this is the printing position. Ink is poured on the screen and pushed through the non-obstructed apertures in the mesh by the pressure and forwards movement, whether it be manual or mechanical, of the squeegee. The screen is then raised and simultaneously re-inked as the squeegee is brought back to its starting point; this operation is known as "flood-coating". The print is removed and placed in a drying rack. The cycle is repeated as many times as there are prints in the edition (multiplied by the number of colours on the print).

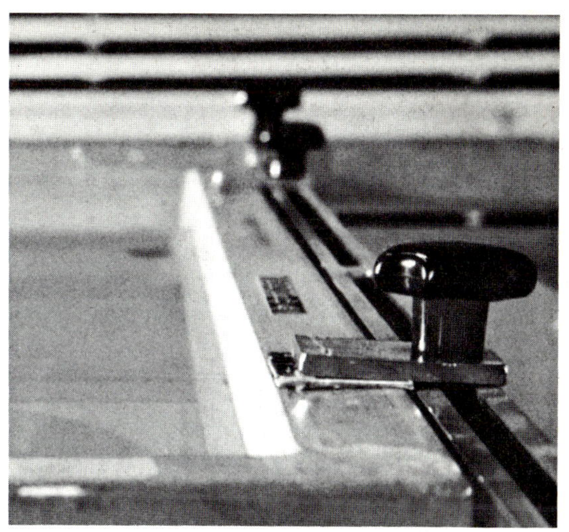

Typical machine-printing hinges

The hand press

As we have seen, the hand press is composed of two essential parts, the base and the hinge mechanism. An adequate base must meet a certain number of precise conditions which will guarantee good

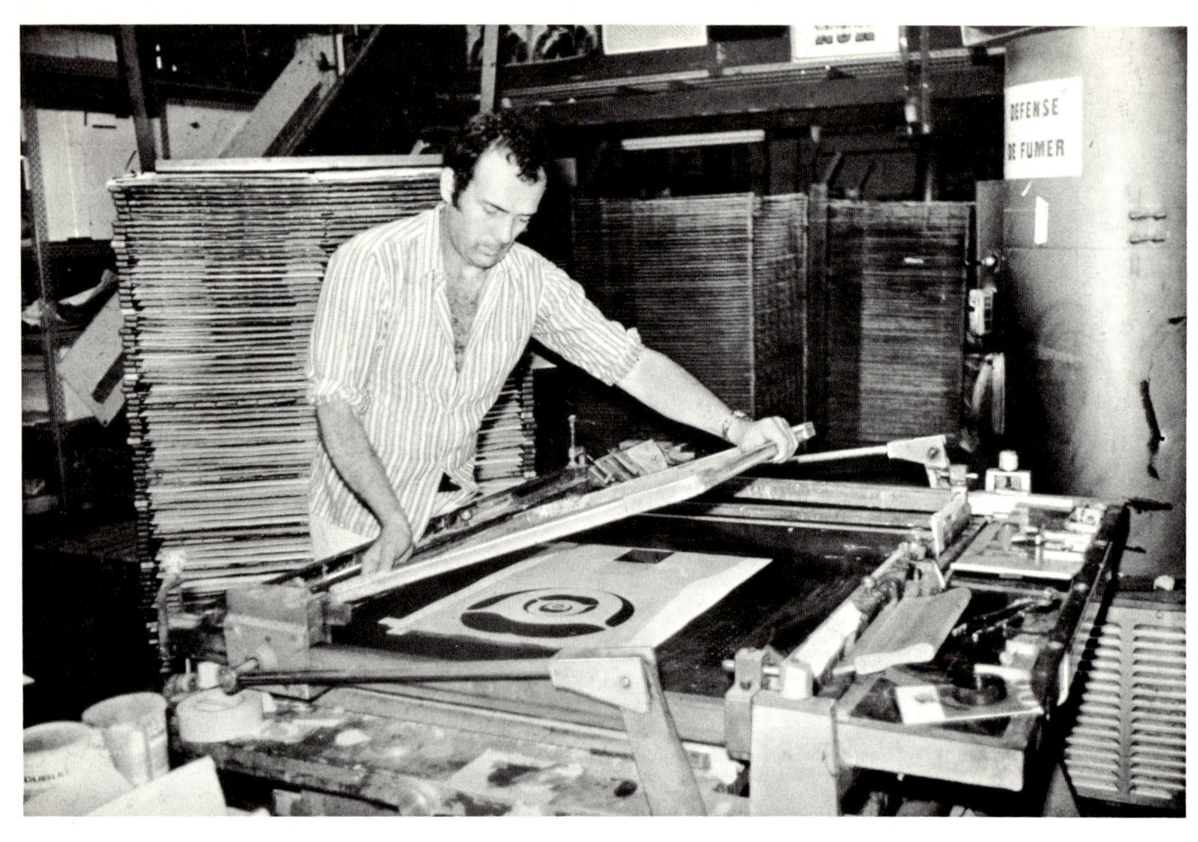

The screen is attached to a press

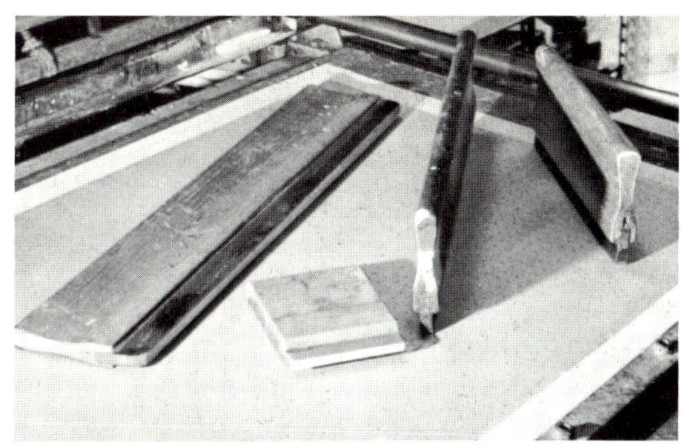

Hand squeegees

quality results: it must be level and rigid, and made of solvent-resistant material (laminate, dural aluminium or steel), and above all, it should be a "*vacuum table*", in other words pierced with hundreds of small holes leading to an air-tight box in which a partial vacuum is created during the printing part of the cycle, strong enough to hold the sheet of paper against the base. This partial vacuum is automatically released when the screen is raised, permitting an easy registration of the next sheet. If the paper is not held solidly in place on the base during printing, a combination of phenomena including the suction and capillary attraction of the ink and, often, static electricity, may cause it to stick to the underside of the screen, or, worse still, having been detached from it, to curl up and stick to it again, the final result being a smudged, messy print. Furthermore, air displaced when the screen is lowered is liable to move the paper just before printing, rendering any accurate registration impossible.

The partial vacuum is obtained with a high-speed rotary turbine pump of between $^1/_2$ and 1 $^1/_2$ horsepower.

The hinge, that indispensable link between the screen and base, permits the screen to be held in two positions: lowered during printing, raised during flood-coating and while the sheet of paper is changed. Good quality hinges are essential—a wide range is available on the market—because the screen must have no "play" whatsoever, in any direction or position, but specially during printing: with each new sheet of paper the screen must drop back into exactly the same position as before, otherwise accurate registration is once again impossible. Hinges can be very simple, or extremely

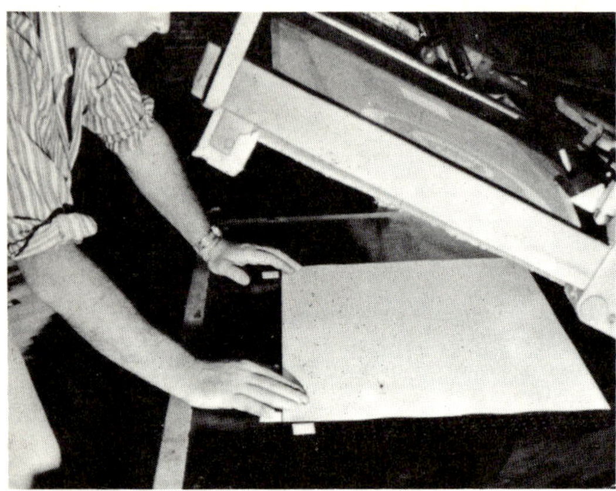

Registering a sheet of paper in the guides

refined with adjustable counterbalance weights, vertical adjustment mechanisms, fine micrometer-screw registration, etc.; screens either clip on to them or are simply held by bolts screwed into threaded sockets in the frame.

The squeegee

This is a most important tool, as it performs the central role of pressing the ink through the screen. The shape, relative hardness and sharpness of the squeegee are responsible for the quality of the print and the thickness of the layer of ink.

The hand-printing squeegee generally consists of a handle made of hardwood or aluminium which is shaped to fit the printer's hand. A rubber or synthetic blade is screwed or glued into the handle, projecting about an inch out from it. The blade should be between $^1/_4$ in. and $^3/_8$ in. thick; its degree of spring can vary greatly. It is worth investing in a complete set of squeegees with different degrees of spring; the length of the squeegee should be such that it clears the printed image by about two inches either side and it should be at least four inches shorter than the interior dimension of the frame. Blades are subject to mechanical wear by being pushed across the fabric under pressure, and are also attacked by the solvents contained in inks. The "edge" is the first to suffer and tends to become rounded. Rubber blades need grinding sharp after about every thousand proofs, whereas synthetic polyurethane can last up to ten times longer. The five types of edge usually ground are, seen in cross-section: right angle, slightly rounded, rounded semi-circle, one side bevelled, both sides bevelled. The classical cross-section

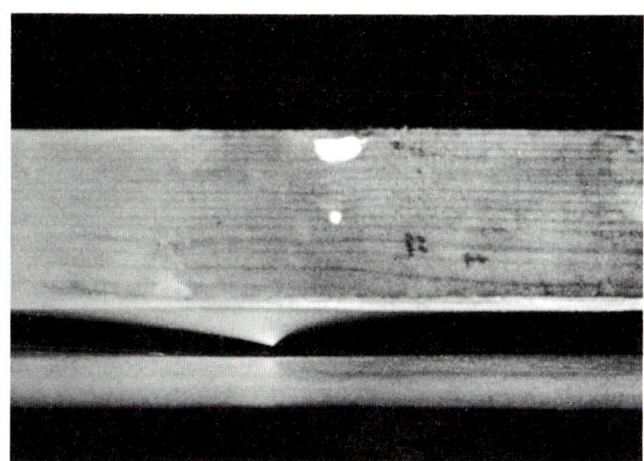

Clearance

for printing on paper is the sharp right-angle. Several types of machine have been manufactured to sharpen squeegees, but they are relatively costly; artists usually just grind the blade against a fairly fine sheet of emery paper, using a guide-rail to maintain the grinding angle at a constant 90°.

Registration and maintaining registration
Registration is a question of determining the position of a colour on the sheet of paper and in relation to the other colours making up the print.

To start with, a general sketch or "master drawing" is made on one of the sheets of paper which will be used for the edition. A classical method of registration is now to draw two or four very neat crosses in the margin; these are transferred to all the screens or transparent positives of all the colours in the print. These crosses are then printed on a certain number of control sheets which will be referred to throughout the edition: all that is now necessary is to make the crosses coincide perfectly for each new colour. They are filled in on the screen before printing the rest of the proofs (the edition). Once the position of the sheet on the base has been decided it must be kept constant throughout the edition and for each colour. So the sheet too must be registered. In screen printing an arrangement of three guides or *stops* is fixed round the "good" corner of the paper, usually the bottom right-hand corner of the sheet being printed, which is commonly registered sideways. The dimensions and positions of these stops must never vary from the start of printing until the edition is completed, nor between colours.

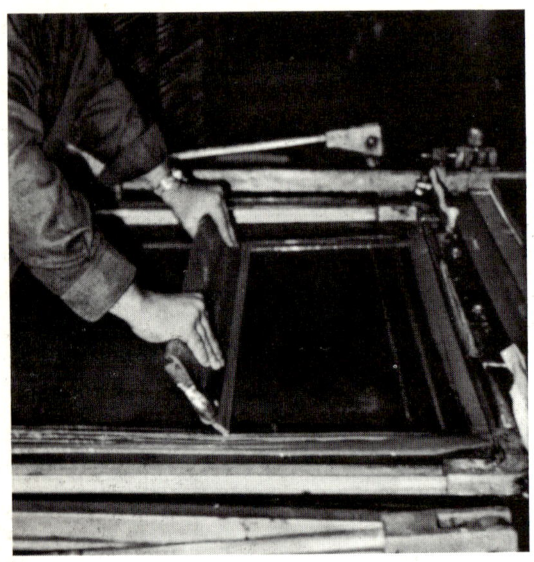

The ideal squeegee angle for hand-printing: 50°

There are all sorts of stops; the simplest are often the best: small strips of self-adhesive plastic stuck to the base.

The relative transparency of the screen is of great help to registration. If a printing table incorporating a precision micrometer-screw registration system is being used, the screen is put roughly in position, then the final adjustment is carried out using the micrometer-screw. To keep this registration constant various other factors must be taken into consideration: the screens should all be of the same size, equally stretched and made of the same fabric; the speed, angle and pressure of the squeegee must also remain constant; finally the clearance between the mesh and the paper should not change from one colour to the next or while printing the same colour. Unfortunately, despite all these precautions, some stretching or shrinkage of the paper is often noticeable, particularly if it takes several days to print the edition.

Clearance

As we have said above, when the frame is lowered onto the printing paper the mesh should lie parallel to the sheet but slightly clear of it. The purpose of this is to prevent the paper from becoming stuck to the mesh after the squeegee has been pushed across the screen, and thus obtain a clear, neat, first class print. It is important not to forget that clearance causes some distension of the mesh when the squeegee is pushed across with the pressure necessary to force the mesh down onto the paper to deposit a coat of ink. So if the clearance is altered during the printing of a colour or between colours, the dimensions of the image will alter and the quality of the registration will suffer. Once the clearance has been decided, then, it must not be changed. Some bases are equipped with screws level with the ends of the screen frame with which the clearance can be precisely set. Otherwise it can be achieved by glueing small strips of cardboard under the frame.

How to print

Now the screen is in position, the registration has been prepared, the squeegee chosen and the ink is ready. What remains to be done is to block out the border of the screen to prevent ink from seeping between the mesh and the inside edge of the frame. Strips of adhesive tape made watertight with a coat of stopping-out liquid will seal up the screen effectively. The printing process itself can be divided into five stages:

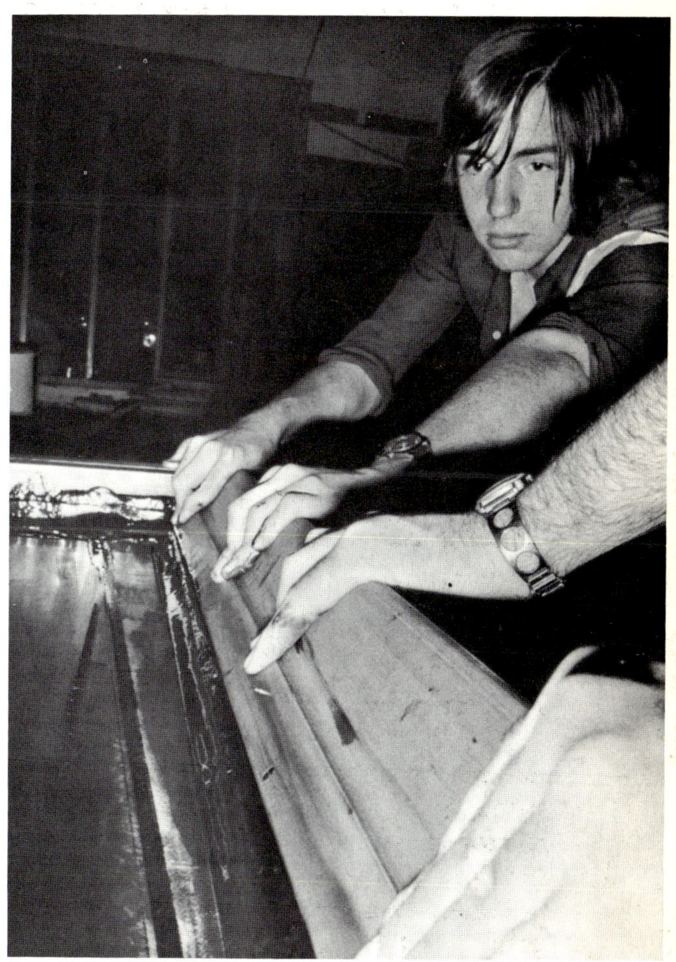

Pulling a giant print

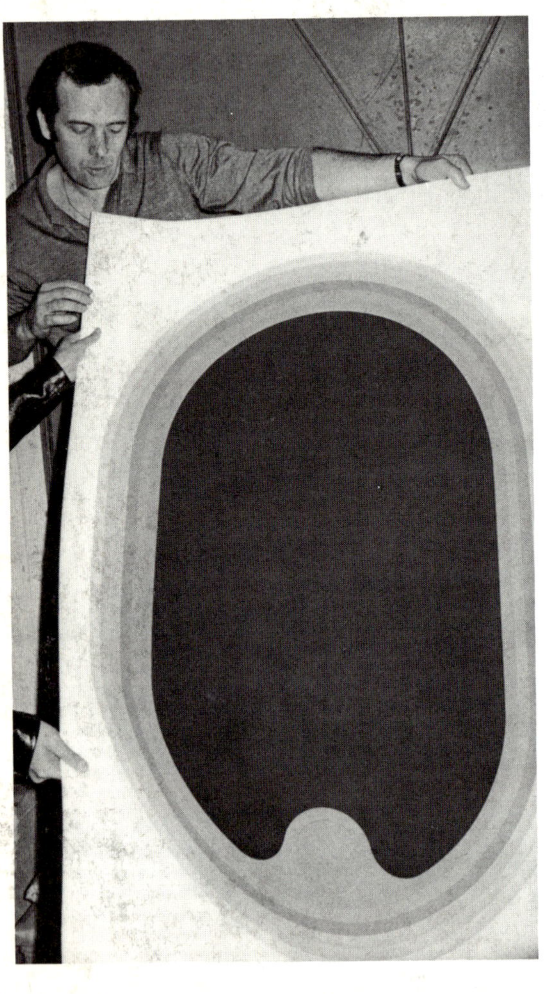

1. With the screen raised, the first sheet of paper is placed against the registration stops.

2. The screen is lowered onto the base.

3. A *pool* of ink is separated from the *well* with the squeegee which the printer then pulls towards him, applying pressure downwards at an angle of between 40 and 55°. The angle and speed of the pull should remain as constant as possible from one side of the frame to the other. The best way to find the correct speed is to observe the way the ink becomes "disengaged" from the mesh. To obtain a clear print the mesh must "snap up" from the paper immediately behind the working edge of the squeegee and no later. As for the best angle—it is found by practice; but as a general rule one may say that a squeegee pulled at too flat an angle will tend to deposit too thick a coat of ink, which will result in a fuzzy print, while too vertical an angle will cause a weak coating with gaps. The correct pressure depends on so many factors that it can only be determined by the printer's

Giant print

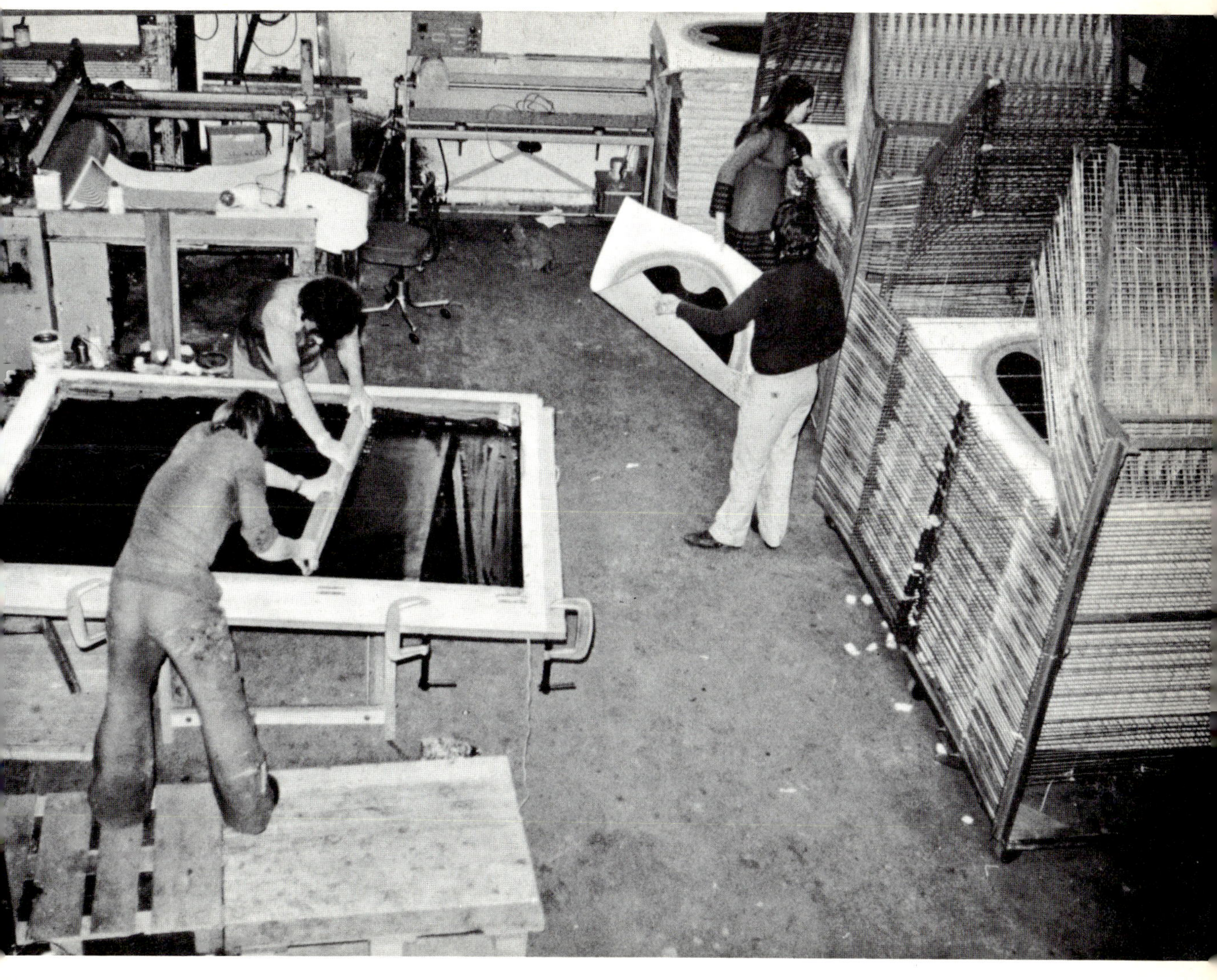

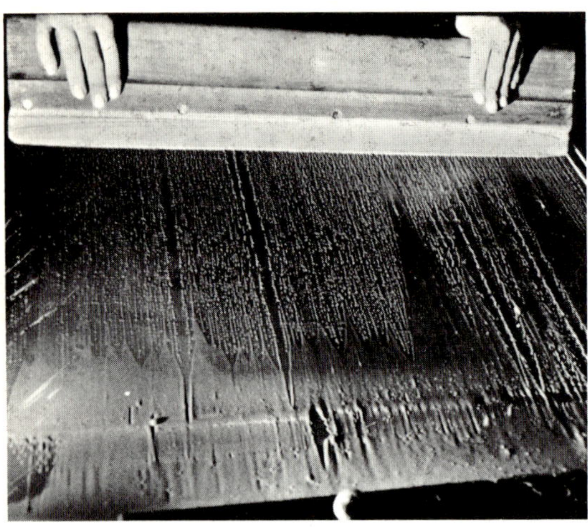

Droplets left by the squeegee: a typical printing error

"instinct", acquired by training and experience. Although theoretically the squeegee stroke can be in any direction: pushed or pulled, from left to right or right to left, the most efficient movement is also the most natural: pulling the squeegee back from the farthest edge towards the body.

4. The printer raises the screen with one hand, and with the other pushes the squeegee and pool of ink back towards the hinges, covering the whole surface of the mesh with a thin coat of ink. This operation—flood-coating—ensures a good deposit of ink for the next pull. On semi-manual machines it is carried out automatically by a "counter-squeegee", normally made of metal, while the screen is raised.

5. The proof is removed from the stops and laid in the drying rack, then a fresh sheet of paper is taken and the five stages are begun again.

Possible printing mishaps

A certain number of minor mishaps may occur during printing. Small drops of ink can slip under the squeegee and mark the proof; these are removed by stopping the ink with a quick movement of the wrist. Failure of some areas to print is sometimes caused by lack of pressure on the squeegee during printing or else by poor flood-coating. Bubbles on the surface of the ink after a pull suggest that the ink was mixed too rapidly during its preparation. There exist anti-bubble and anti-froth additives to prevent this. Clouded effects and uneven inking are caused by insufficient tension of the mesh, or by a brutal and late "snap up" of the mesh well after the squeegee has passed. If a previous colour has not been cleaned off the screen thoroughly enough, traces of hardened ink, emulsion or stopping-out liquid give rise to unwanted ghostly images which keep reappearing throughout the edition. Finally, dust in the atmosphere, or from the paper, sticking to the underside of the screen imparts a fuzzy blotched effect to fine lines: so the lower surface of the screen should be cleaned gently from time to time with a solvent, not only because of the dust collected under the mesh but also to prevent the printed proof from becoming "restuck" to the screen—because static electricity can trouble the printer too. Electrical devices designed to eliminate it are costly and still not perfect, but on the other hand there are anti-static products on the market which can be added to the ink or applied to the screen from time to time when suitable.

Drying

As we have seen, ink takes some time to dry; and in screen printing wet colours are

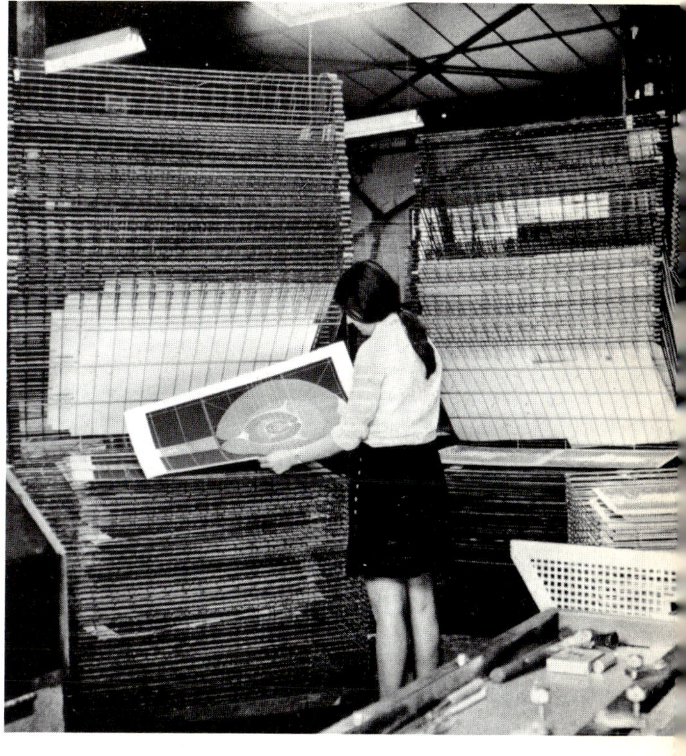

Drying racks

never superimposed, excepting dyes for printing fabrics. A proof must thus be perfectly dry before the next colour is pulled. Although numerous (and very expensive) hot air, infra-red, ultra-short wave or other drying machines are available, the best way to dry proofs remains exposure to ordinary air. Devices for drying are fairly simple to set up, but it is worth investing in a couple of metal drying racks. Half-inch spaces between the frames allow for good drying, particularly if some gentle ventilation can be arranged about a yard above ground-level, which is the maximum accumulation point of solvent fumes during evaporation. Depending on the nature of the inks and their intrinsic drying speeds, proofs can take between twenty minutes and several hours to dry. When the prints feel thoroughly dry to the touch, they are removed from the drying rack and piled up ready to be printed with the next colour.

Cleaning and recuperating the screen

In the chapter devoted to stencil-making we saw how to remove the various films, emulsions, stopping-out liquids, etc., with appropriate solvents or hot water and concentrated sodium hypochlorite. Cleaning off inks is equally important; a screen which has been printing with glycerophthalic ink, for instance, if imperfectly cleaned after an edition, must be considered as permanently lost.

First any ink left on the screen should be scooped off with an offcut of cardboard or a flat metal spatula. The screen is then placed on a pile of old newspapers and a solvent suitable for the ink used is poured into the frame. Some solvents—a solution of toluene and 5 % ethyl acetate, for instance—will dissolve nearly all screen inks. Both sides of the screen are rubbed with rags or cellulose wadding impregnated with solvent until all traces of ink have dissolved and disappeared completely. This operation must be repeated until no trace of colour comes off on the rag used for rubbing.

Yaakov Agam, La Thora, *1971. 98 colour screen print*

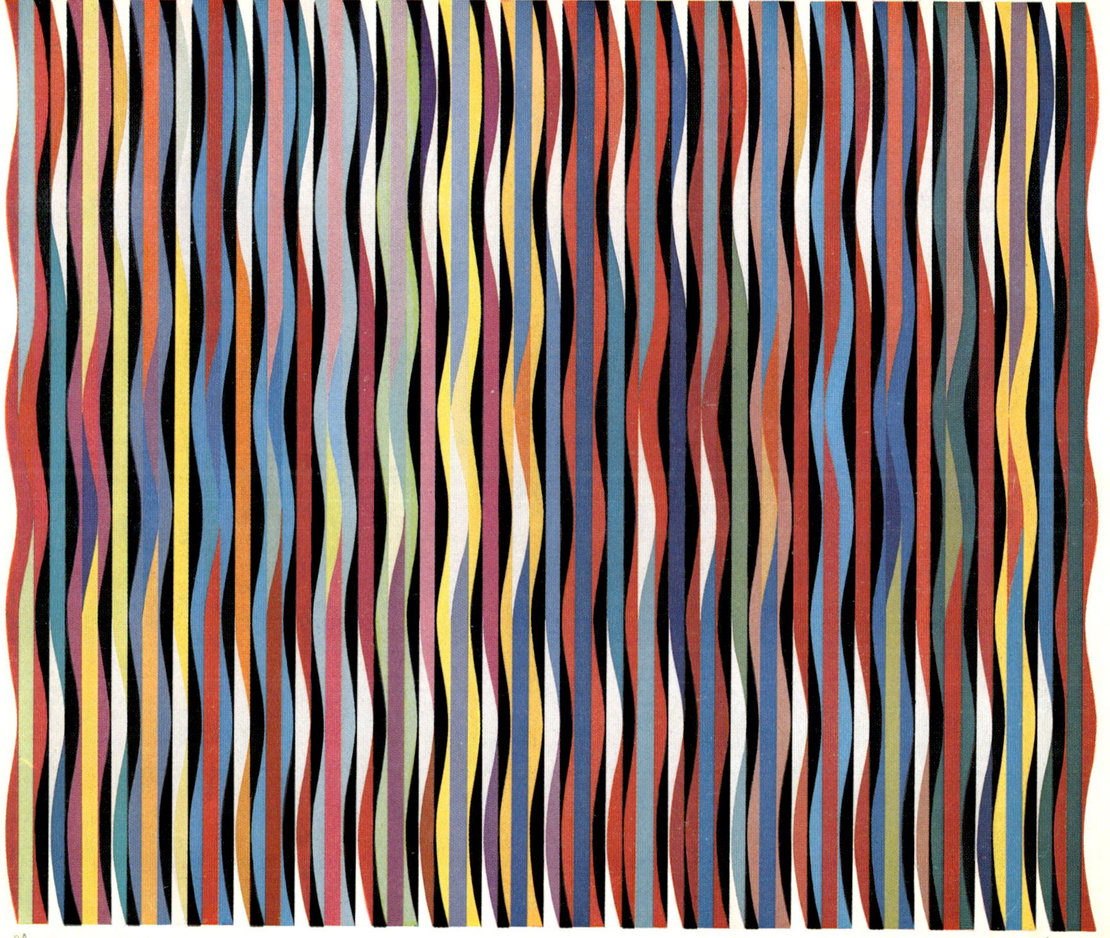

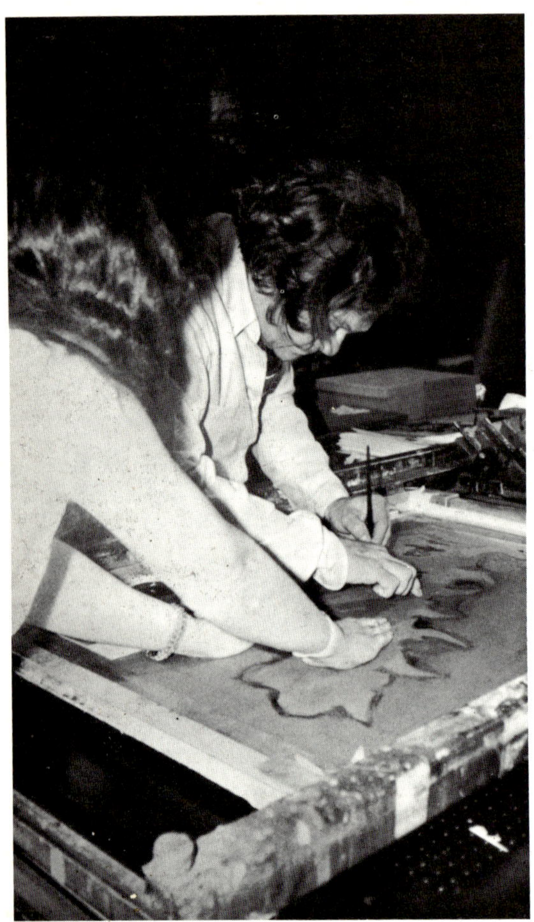

Daniel Milhaud working directly on a screen

6 THE ARTIST AND THE SCREEN PRINTER

Most original screen prints are the result of an intimate collaboration between an artist and a professional screen printer. The artist, after preparing screens directly or the stencils to be transferred to them, in his own studio or in the silk screen workshop, later supervises work at the printing table, making sure that his instructions on colours and the qualities of ink and printing are followed, even if he does not pull the proofs himself.

The principal task of the screen printer is to adapt himself easily to the style and taste of the artist with whom he teams up. He must also provide him with detailed guidance and advice on how "technique" can be made to serve and enrich the artist's ideas rather than limit them.

Back at the printing table a printer pulls a certain number of "trial proofs" for the artist, first on newsprint then on the paper intended for the edition. It is on these proofs that the registration of the different colours, the colour tonality desired and the superimposition of transparent colours are all worked out precisely. The artist also sees if it is necessary to retouch the screen in any way. When satisfied with the result, the artist gives his "o.k.", if necessary signing the most successful trial proof.

Trial proofs being sometimes unique—monotypes, in a way—are often much prized by collectors. They illustrate the artist's intellectual and aesthetic processes at work, his tentative essays, his hesitations and occasionally even his belated changes of mind. They are, in a way, the questions and answers of his graphic research. Because of the relatively speedy execution possible with screen printing, an artist can experiment with colour faster and further than in any other graphic technique.

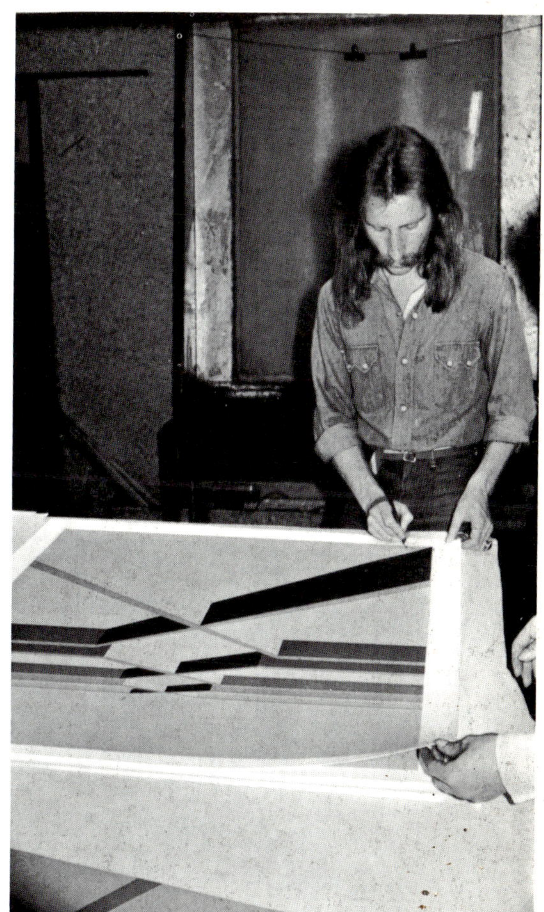

Maxime Deffert signing proofs

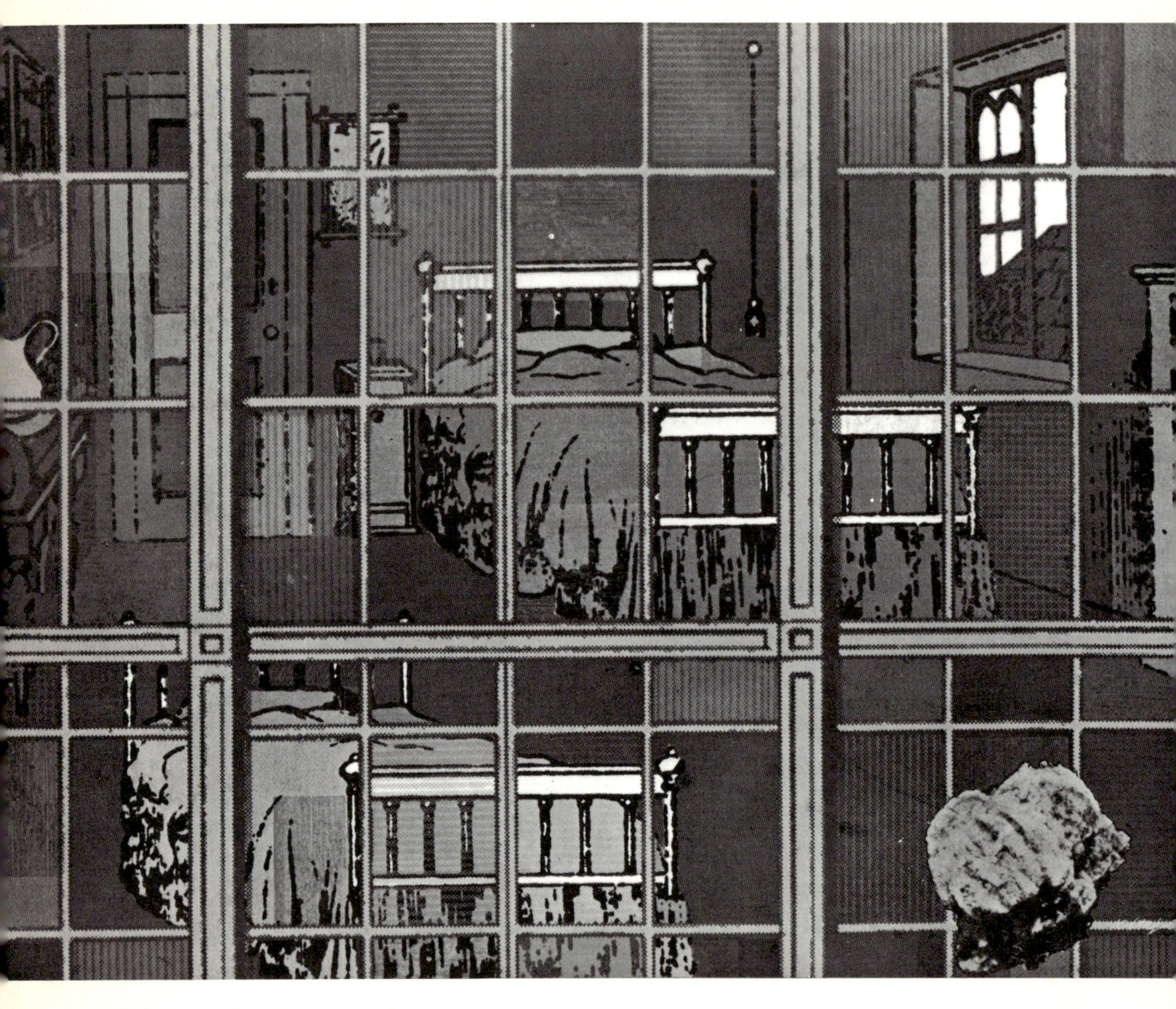

7 VARIATIONS

It is precisely the flexibility, complexity and almost endless possibilities of screen printing that make it possible to carry experimentation with materials and special effects so far. Although this field is wide open to the artist's imagination, there are nevertheless a certain number of "classical" variations which are not lacking in interest.

For example, there is the use of "subjacent" material: a few years ago the variation known as the "string" technique was all the rage; it consisted in working out a design with lengths of string of different widths which were glued directly onto the base. A sheet of thin printing paper was then placed in its stops *over* the string and a flat coat of transparent ink was pulled over it, strong pressure being applied with the squeegee. Very interesting effects of graduated colour were thus obtained, as the ink tended to accumulate in, and so darken, the hollow parts of the paper. Similarly, cut-out card shapes, woodcuts and linocuts and even engraved copper, steel or zinc plates can be arranged on the bed. The paper for this technique can either be used dry, or moistened as for engraving.

Curious coloured texture effects can be obtained by mixing chemically incompatible inks, as long as the "precipitation" is not overdone (in which case the inks become unmanageable): for example a mixture of cellulose and glycerophthalic inks can produce a sort of "hammered" effect or interesting grains. It is also possible to screen print a coating of liquid glue or very thick varnish, which, while still wet and sticky, is powdered with sand or fine gravel, or "flocked" with a fine chaff of rayon fibres manufactured for the purpose. This operation can be carried out

R. B. Kitaj, Bedroom, *1971. Colour screen print*

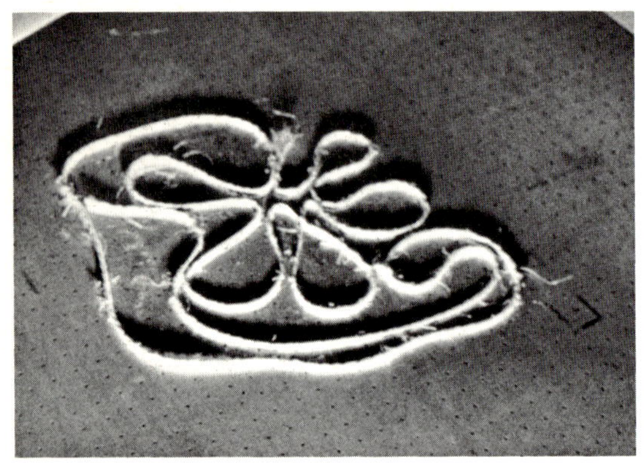

Glueing string to the base

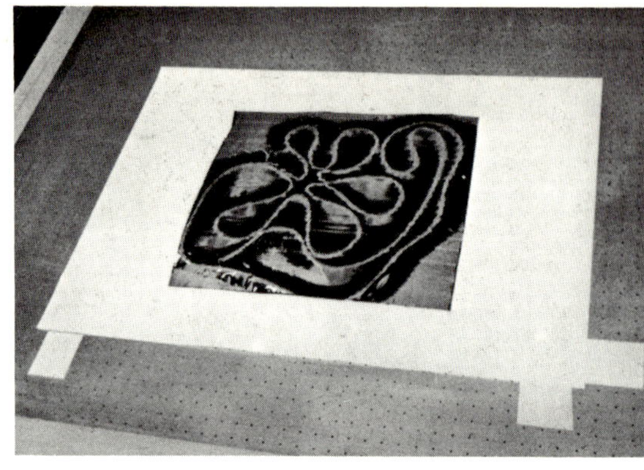

A print

by hand (simply by powdering), with a spray-gun or with the help of special devices operating on static electricity.

Of course there remain all the photographic effects that we mentioned earlier: solarization, line-photo, equi-densities, etc., amongst these "stage-by-stage printing" is a useful way of converting a flat tone into half-tones. 5 or 6 line-positives are made from an ordinary negative with a shorter exposure each time. The darkest positives, which have been exposed the longest, are printed with light-coloured inks, those with the shortest exposure, with dark inks. A single half-tone positive can be used, in another variation of the same principle, to obtain screens blocked out to varying degrees depending simply on the length of exposure. A black and white half-tone negative can also be printed in colour.

"Monotypes" can be made by a screen printing process: the artist draws directly on a clean screen with ink, or several

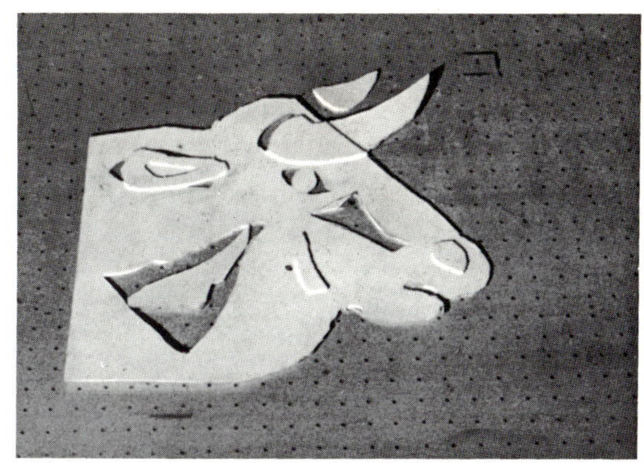

Glueing cut-out card shapes to the base

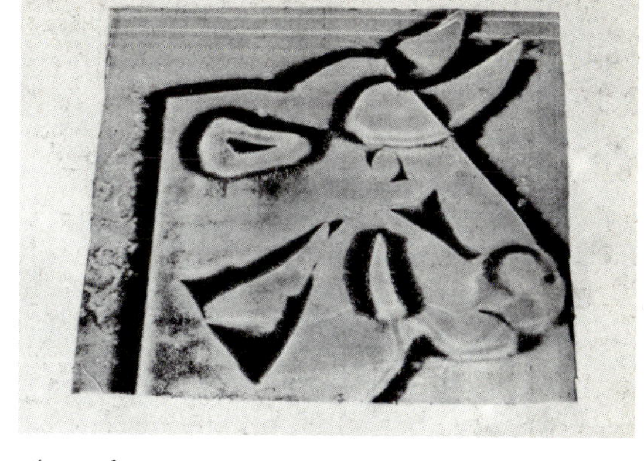

A proof

coloured inks, over which, he can, if he likes, apply a flat coat of another colour with a squeegee or coating trough. He then pulls two or three proofs, which are, of course, different from each other. The colours are mingled by the squeegee stroke, producing certain effects which may well be rather unexpected, but which cannot be obtained by classical drawing and painting techniques.

Original "multiples"—one or several pre-established stencils are printed with a different colour for each proof—are also very easily obtained by silk screen.

Finally, of course, as many artists intent on exploiting to the full the particularities of all the various original graphic reproduction processes have demonstrated, silk screen can well be "married" with engraving, lithography, woodcuts and linocuts, copper-plate, etc.

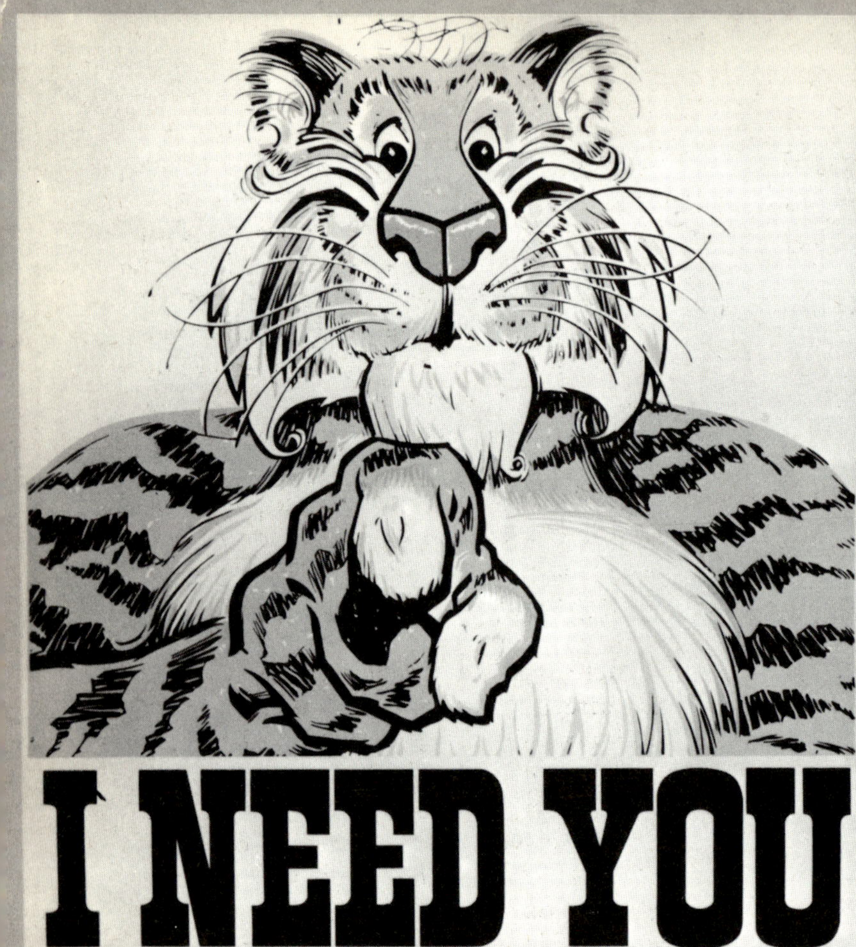

Screen print advertisement

8 SILK SCREEN IN ADVERTISING, DECORATION AND INDUSTRY

In many fields, and particularly in the field of graphic art, our "hyper-industrialized, soberly logical, above all practical and absurdly over-mechanized . . ." society, can be observed behaving in one of two ways: it either relegates an expressive art to the condition rather disparagingly qualified as "fine old craftsmanship", or it takes it over completely to "rationalize" it into an industrial technique. Thus lithography gave birth to offset, gravure to heliogravure, wood engraving to typography and silk screen to the industrial screen process.

There is as much difference between a silk screen hand printing table and the machines which print, say, 4,000 bottles an hour or spew forth 3,000 yards of cloth an hour, printed in 8 colours in immediate succession, as there is between the lithographic hand press, from which three or four needle-registered proofs can be coaxed in an hour and an offset machine knocking off 10,000 examples in the same period of time. Nevertheless, both tables and machines are based on the same silk screen process.

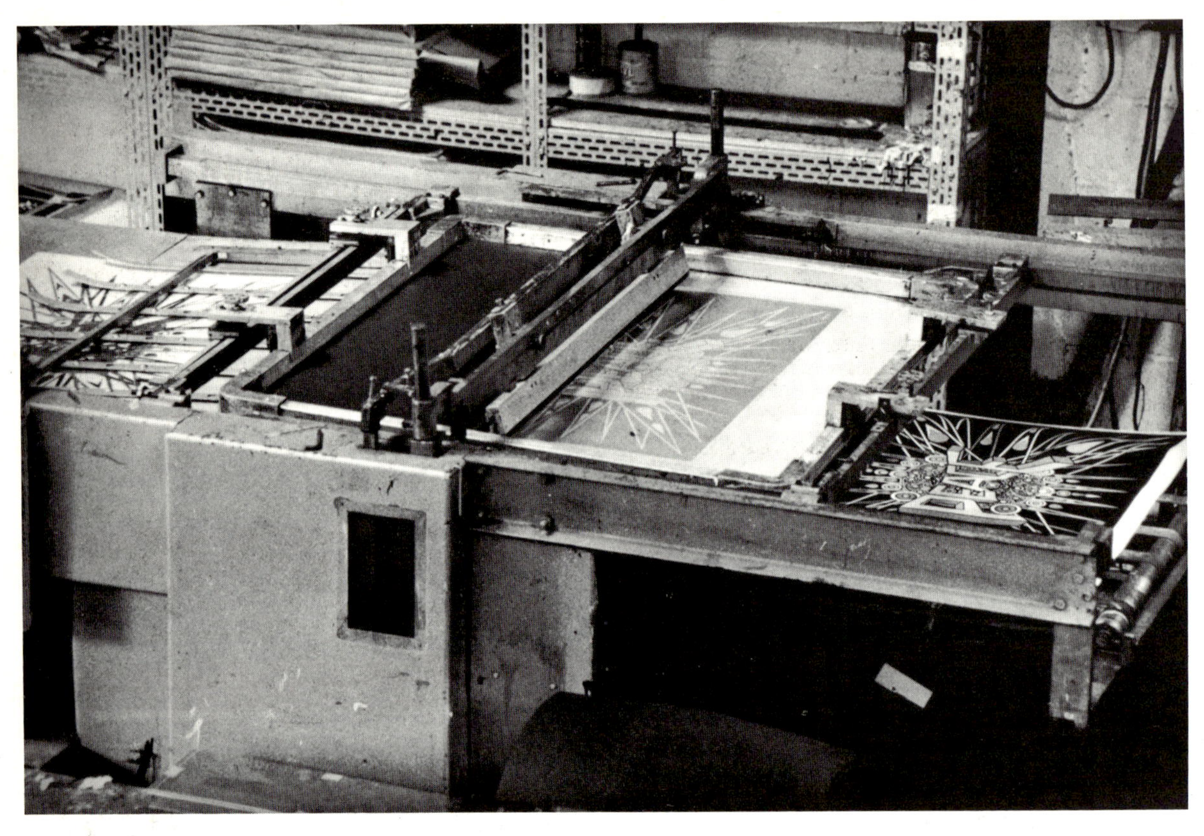

Machine with automatic paper replacement

Although, in its field, silk screen is still often considered as very much a "handicraft" technique, it has at its disposal entirely automatic machines which print and dry 3,000 examples an hour. It is not unusual to see side by side in the same workshop a hand press and a mass production automatic cylindrical press. Although in France silk screen has only captured 5 % of the printing market, in Great Britain, Germany, the United States and Scandinavia it is more like 15 %. In Sweden, for instance, 80 % of outdoor posters are screen-printed, including four-colour reproductions of colour-photos. Both in Europe and in the United States the rapid construction and relatively low cost of the machinery, added to the richness and strength of the printing colours make silk screen the ideal graphic advertising medium for printing very large-format editions of less than 5,000 examples. Being mechanically and chemically highly flexible since it can print on almost any surface using a wide variety of inks, it is the perfect technique for so called "point of sale advertising": shop signs on plastic material, sheet-metal

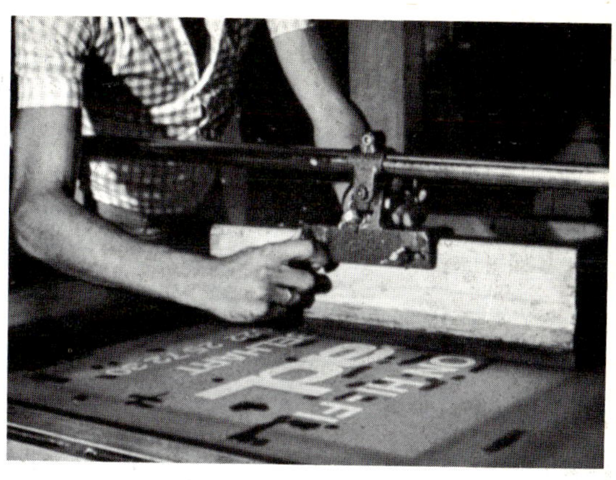

"One hand" press

Semi-automatic or semi-manual press

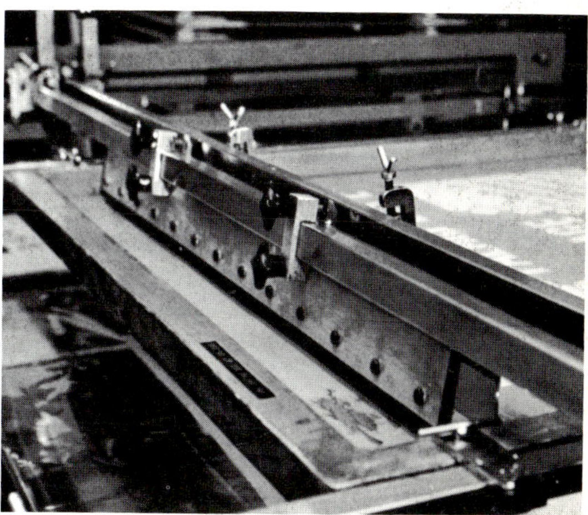

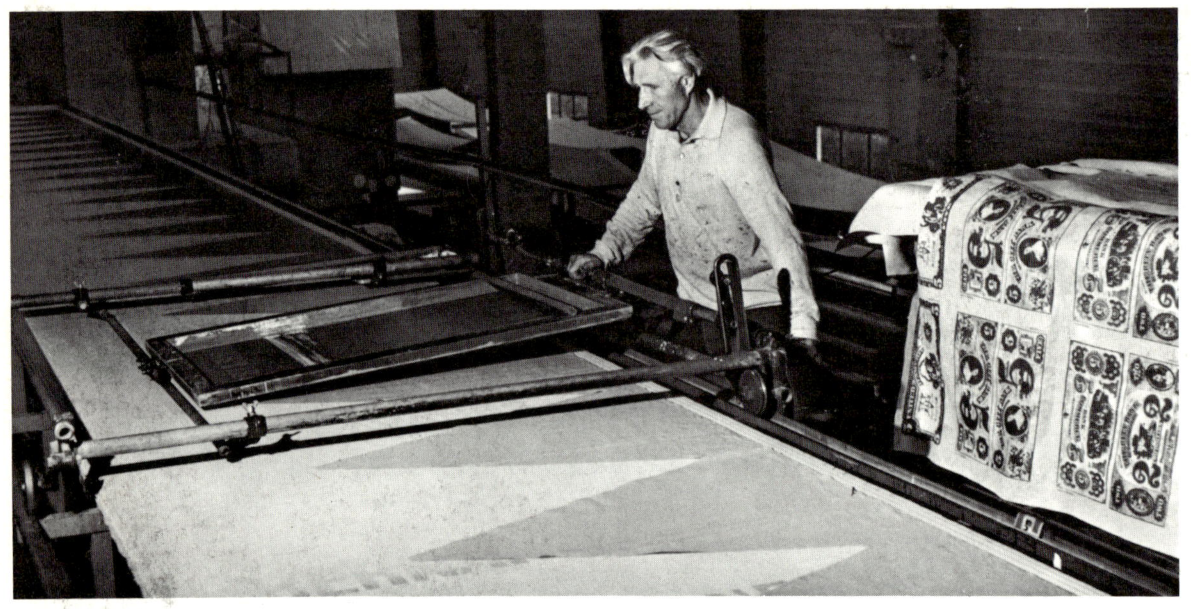

Manual printing "à la lyonnaise"

counter-displays, plastic and cardboard boxes, window displays and store decoration, printed self-adhesive plastic, vitrifiable or simple transfer window stickers, etc.

Quite apart from editions of fine art prints, silk screen is used to print the covers of editions of brochures or books, made in a variety of materials which it would be difficult or impossible to print by other graphic processes. It is also tending to replace its old "ancestor" the stencil, in the illustration of various luxury book editions. Screen printing on paper continues to evolve, in combination with other graphic techniques: in a recent

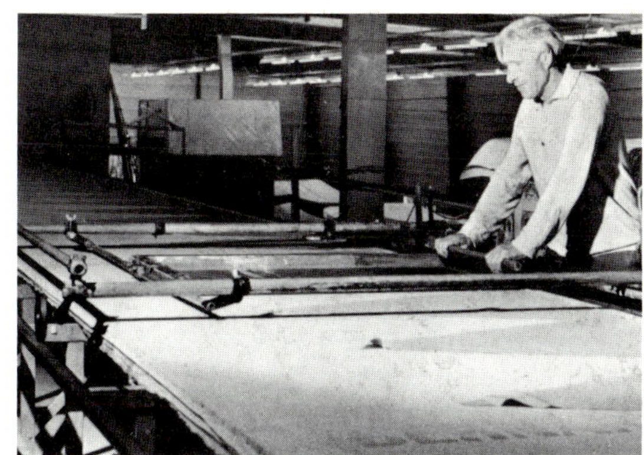

Printing "à la lyonnaise" – pulling

silk screen press the squeegee has been replaced by a device which sucks ink through the paper, and makes it possible to print 20 juxtaposed colours simultaneously with gaps of about $^{3}/_{8}$ in. between them. Combining the principle of Xerography (printing by the attraction exerted on electrically charged particles of colour by modulated magnetic fields) with a silk screen one can dispense with the delicate operation of imparting a differential charge to the underlying plate.

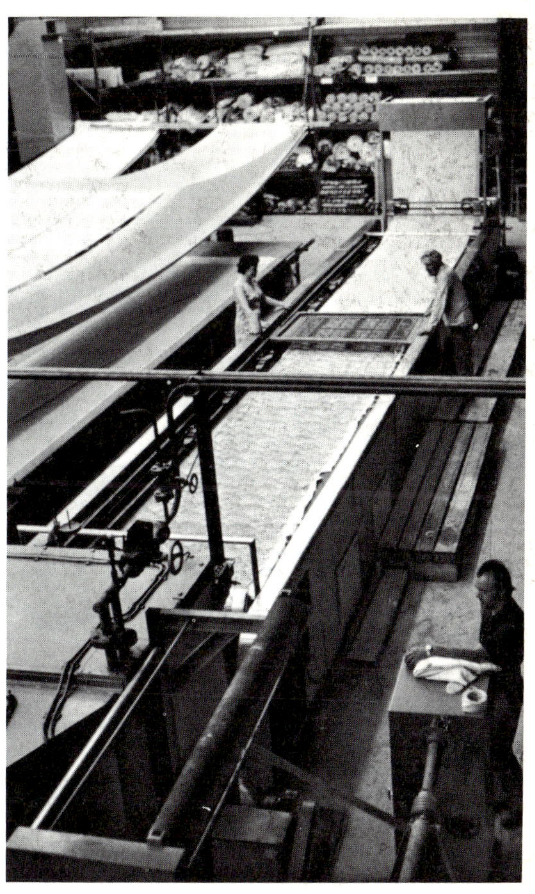

General view of a workshop

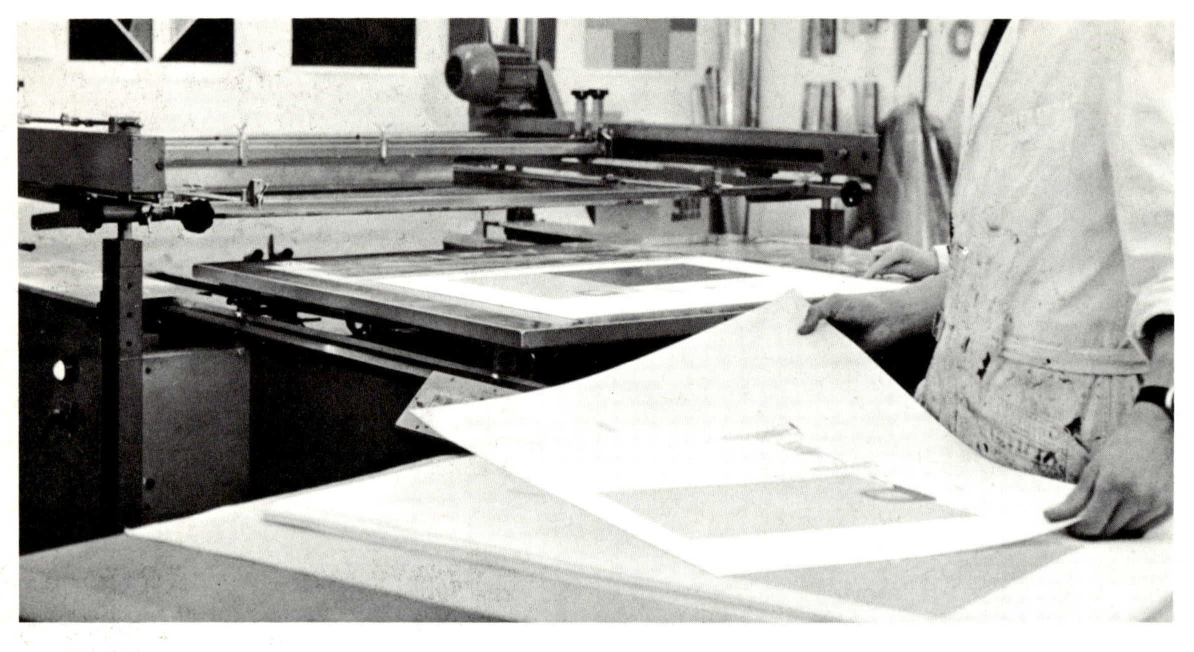

Pulling a screen print on a semi-automatic press

Semi-automatic bottle-printing production line (p. 91) ▷
Printed electronic circuit (p. 91) ▷

Silk screen is very often used, in conjunction with other processes, in all departments of decoration: wall-papers, upholstery fabrics, floor-covering and wall laminates, for example.

We must not forget that silk screen printing was first applied "industrially" in England and France just about one hundred years ago. A fabric printing technique known as "à la Lyonnaise" which was used—at its beginnings—for printing short lengths of expensive silk cloth was inescapably based on the principle of "ink through mesh"—that is to say screen printing. And now that ultra-rapid rotary machines have taken its place for printing very large editions, they too, consisting as they do of chemically perforated metal mesh cylinders, are based on the principle of the silk screen process.

Nevertheless, it is not in the fields of graphics and decoration that screen printing has developed most widely in the last twenty years, but in industrial labelling or marking, especially in printing trade names and instructions on glass. Using fusible glazes which are printed hot through metal screens, up to 4,000 bottles

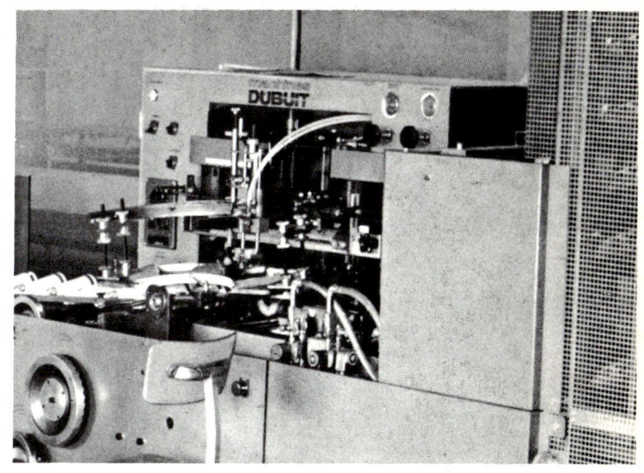

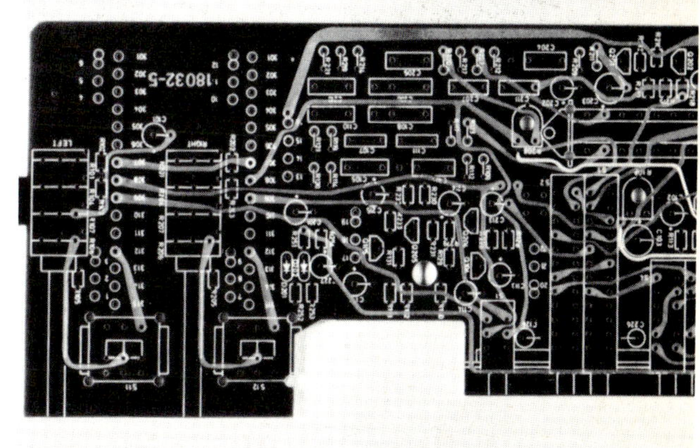

an hour can be printed with 4 colours simultaneously, with glazes of successively lower melting points for each colour in turn. In fact the screen printing process is really "inverted" for printing on cylindrical or conical surfaces: the squeegee blade is fixed, instead of mobile, and it is the screen which moves while the object being printed completes a full revolution. So the printing takes place tangentially to the point where pressure is applied by the fixed squeegee blade. The application of this principle in conjunction with the chemical diversity of screen printing inks has catapulted this process way ahead of the field in plastic bottle printing, even on materials which had been considered unprintable, like the *polyethylenes*. By combining shaped screens and cylindrical machines, it is even feasible to print on entirely spherical surfaces. A host of ultra-specialized screen printing machines has sprung up: some will only print on pencils and ball-point pens, others on lipstick tubes; yogurt pots, barrels, even socks all have their own specialized machines!

Also, it has been found that screen printing is an ideal way of applying a reliable, tough coat of protecting varnish, before, for instance, partially "de-silvering" the surface of a publicity mirror. More often still, it is used to protect certain parts of "printed" electric or electronic circuits with which transistor radios, television sets, control equipment, etc., are now manufactured.

Finally, glaze can be applied directly to pottery, china and earthenware by screen printing, or indirectly, using vitrifiable transfers.

Marc Baumann, Les Paons, *1962. 5 colour seritapestry*

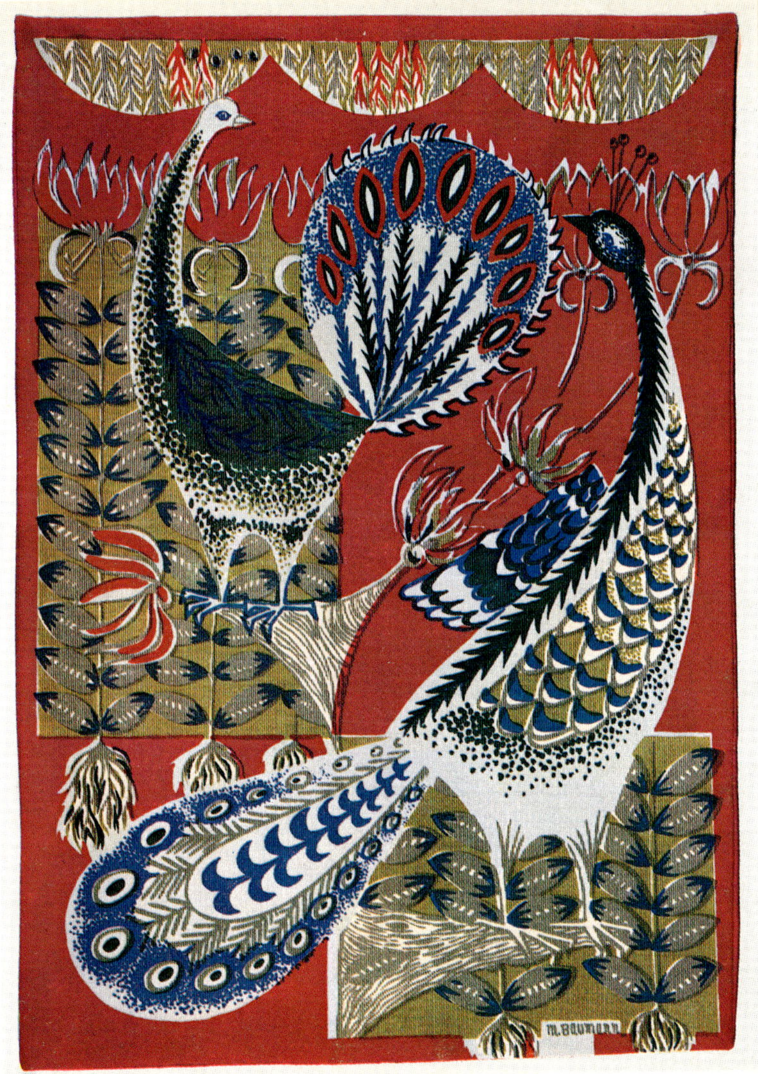

9 THE HISTORY OF SILK SCREEN

Detail from a Chinese screen

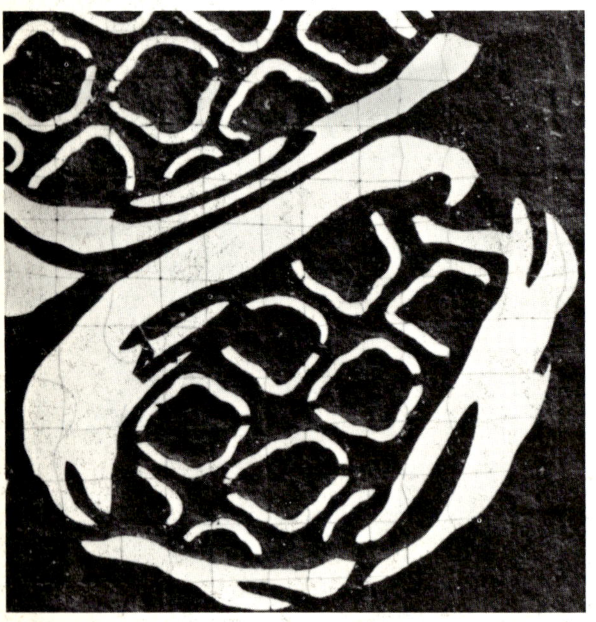

No historian has as yet undertaken a definitive history of silk screen, although sufficient mile-stones of evidence have been unearthed to lead us safely back several centuries.

It seems useless, in any case, to deny the existence of a link between silk screen and the common stencil, which is probably the most ancient of all techniques of graphic expression. Francis Carr, of the London School of Printing, traces stencilling back 30.000 years before our era, citing the black and red friezes of "hands" in the Gargas grottos in the High-Pyrenees: coloured earth blown through a hollow reed around hands spread against the rock—the first stencils! From there, lacking proper historical evidence, we must make a mighty jump forwards to the Roman empire, during the first century of our era. The historian Quintilian describes how children were taught writing with wood stencils to guide their stylets. Roman emperors like Justinian, Goth chieftains like Theodoric (according to

Lola Fernandez, Composition, *1972. 5 colour screen print*

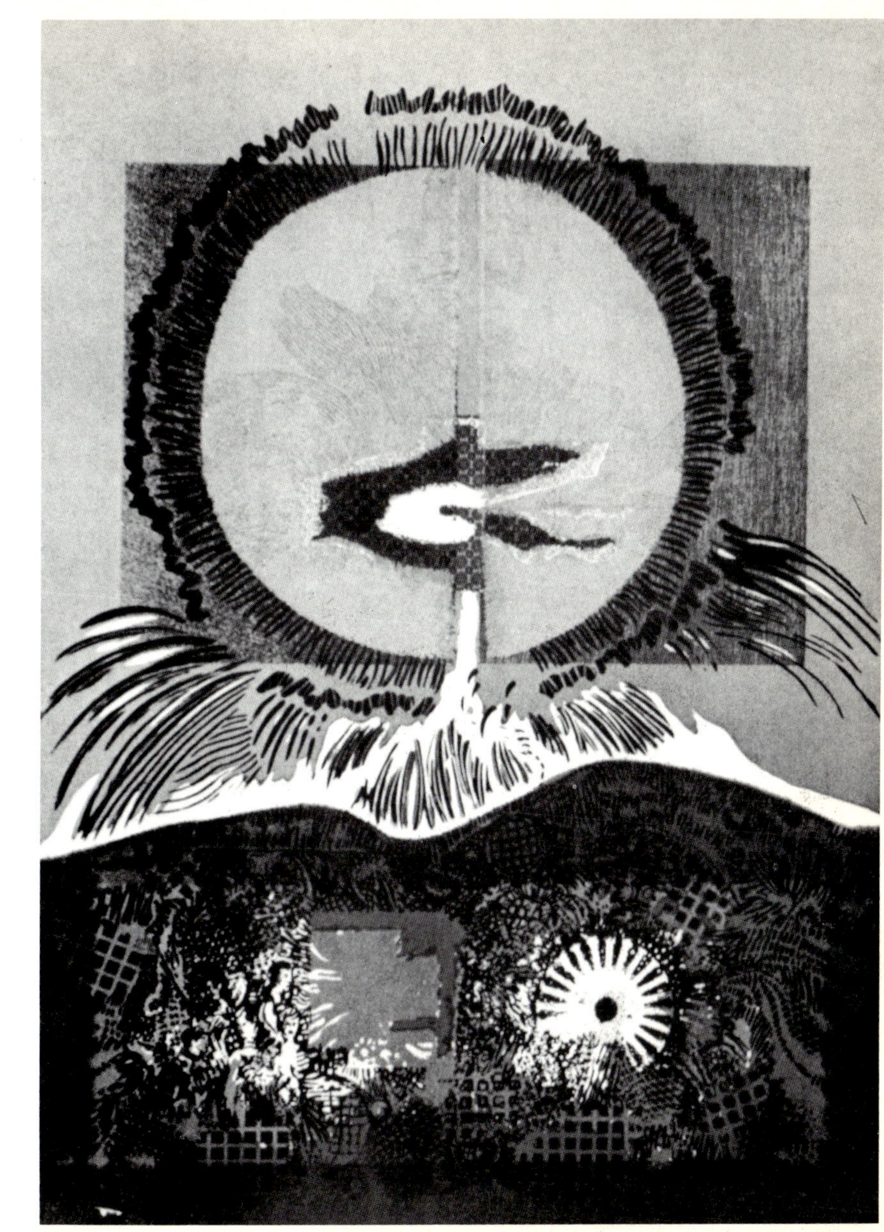

Procopius), and Pope Adrian all signed their initials through perforated plates of copper, gold or ivory. In the Grotto of a Thousand Buddhas, in Tibet, Sir Aurel Stein discovered the stencils which had been used in about the year 500 A.D. to decorate the walls with effigies of Bhuddha. In Japan, ceremonial robes and kimonos have long been decorated with stencils. According to a very ancient tradition this Japanese practice would be the real origin of silk screen.

In the Middle Ages stencilling was an art of the common man, used for decorating playing cards as well as popular or religious imagery; "Briefmaler" in Germany, and in France, "Dominotiers", (playing-card-makers) excelled in the field. It was also much in demand at this period for mural decoration and for printing silk and brocade wall-hangings. The zenith of stencilling, in these different domains, was reached during the 16th and 17th centuries.

In the 18th century, a Frenchman, J. Papillon, printed the first wall papers using a stencil roller, and invented the "domino pattern". At that same period the printing of "Fraktur", the script of Gregorian chant choir-books, was greatly facilitated by the use of stencils.

Epinal prints, which were very much in vogue during the Napoleonic era, were coloured by stencil.

Early in the 20th century stencilling was extremely fashionable, thanks to Claude Saudé in France, William Morris and William Crawhall in England. Nor is the brief but brilliant sally into this field by Olivier Simon, about 1920, likely to be forgotten easily.

Reverting to silk screen printing proper, it seems as if we had better work our way through several centuries back towards Japan, for it looks as if the first silk screen was invented by Some Ya Yu Zen, about the end of the 17th century. It consisted of two sheets of mulberry tree paper made impermeable by oiling; one of these sheets was coated with glue and stuck to a mesh of hair stretched on a card-board frame; the other sheet, cut out in the same way, was perfectly registered and stuck to the first, underneath the mesh. A brush was used to press colour through the stencil. We do not know who first had

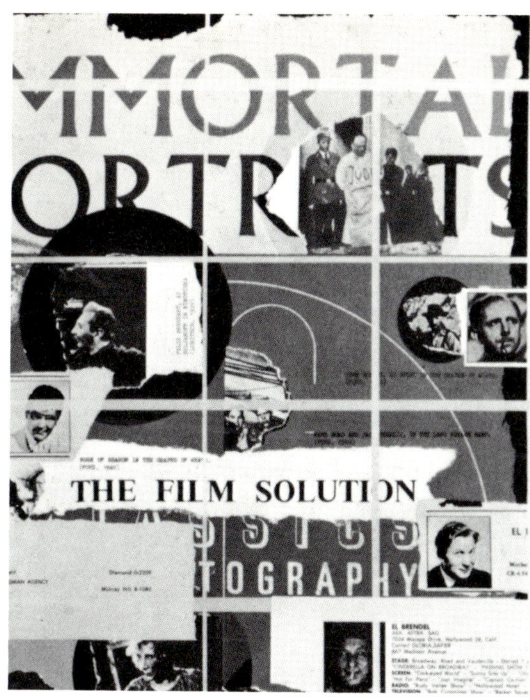

R. B. Kitaj, Immortal Portraits, *1972. Silk screen and collage*

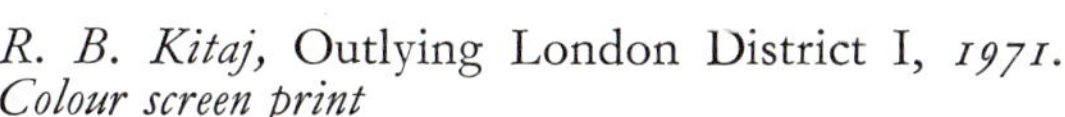

R. B. Kitaj, Outlying London District I, *1971. Colour screen print*

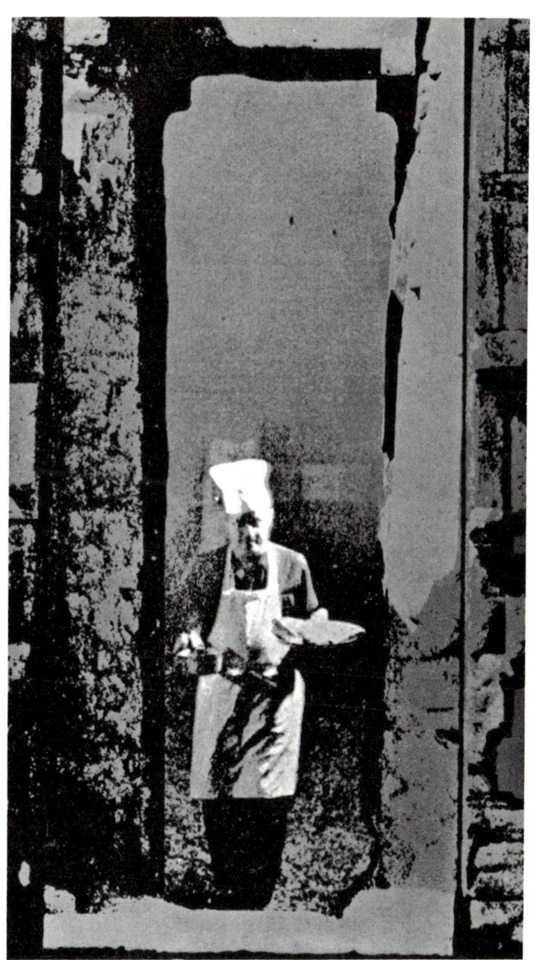

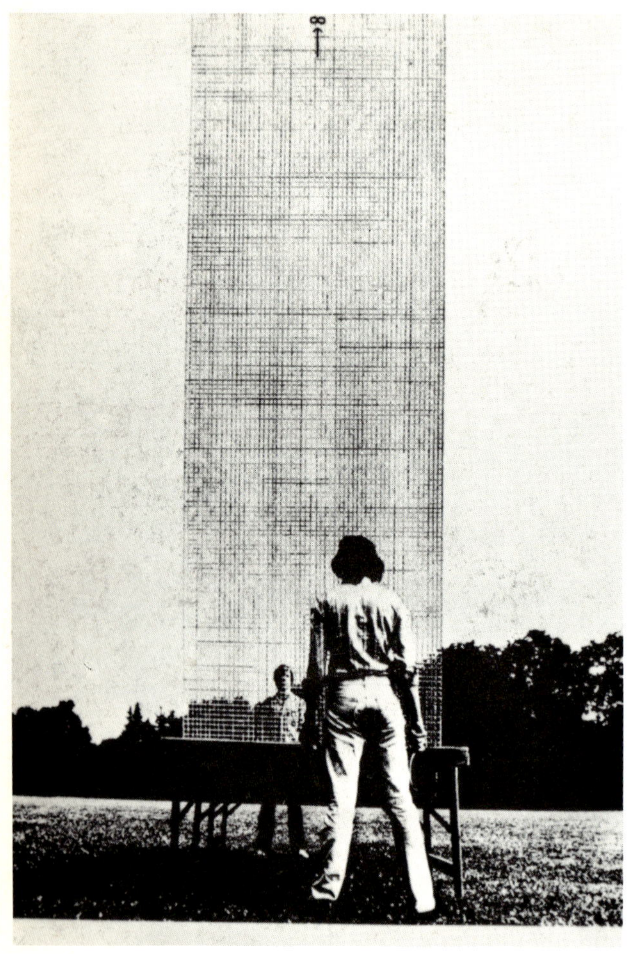

the idea of using a wood frame. But it was in London, in about 1850, that a screen of this sort was first put on display; it triggered off "screen" printing of textiles, both in England and the Lyon region of France.

If we look out for such clear landmarks as patents, we must wait until the year 1907, when one Samuel Simon was granted a patent in Manchester to manufacture a screen of bolting silk stretched on a frame; the drawing technique was direct, using stopping-out liquid, but printing was carried out with a brush.

For thirteen years silk screen printing developed steadily in the United States and Great Britain. It is not known who replaced the brush, first by a felt roller, then by the classical squeegee with a rubber blade. Neither do we know who was the first to print on paper using the silk screen process. In 1920, in Berlin, Albert Kosloff and Biegeleisen gave a demonstration of what they called *Sieb-*

Gérald Ducimetière, Composition, *1972. Black and white screen print*

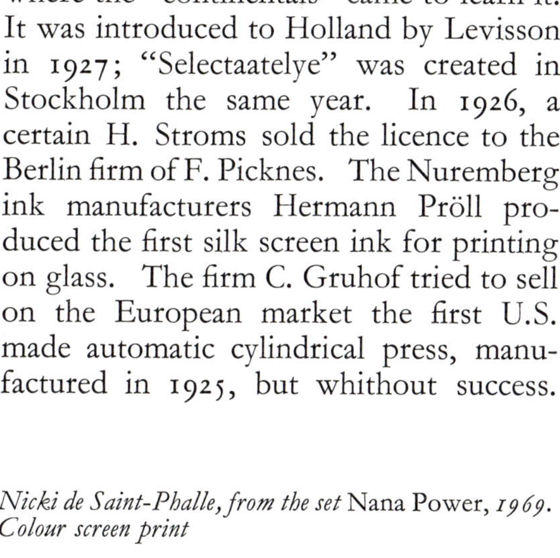

druck, which was in fact silk screen printing, without arousing much interest. Disappointed by this unenthusiastic reception, they emigrated first to England, then to the United States, where they became eminent pioneers of the process and respected university professors. There is one outstanding name in the history of silk screen printing: Selectasine—a method developed in 1923 in San Francisco which was quickly taken up throughout the United States, then, in 1925, in London, where the "continentals" came to learn it. It was introduced to Holland by Levisson in 1927; "Selectaatelye" was created in Stockholm the same year. In 1926, a certain H. Stroms sold the licence to the Berlin firm of F. Picknes. The Nuremberg ink manufacturers Hermann Pröll produced the first silk screen ink for printing on glass. The firm C. Gruhof tried to sell on the European market the first U.S. made automatic cylindrical press, manufactured in 1925, but whithout success.

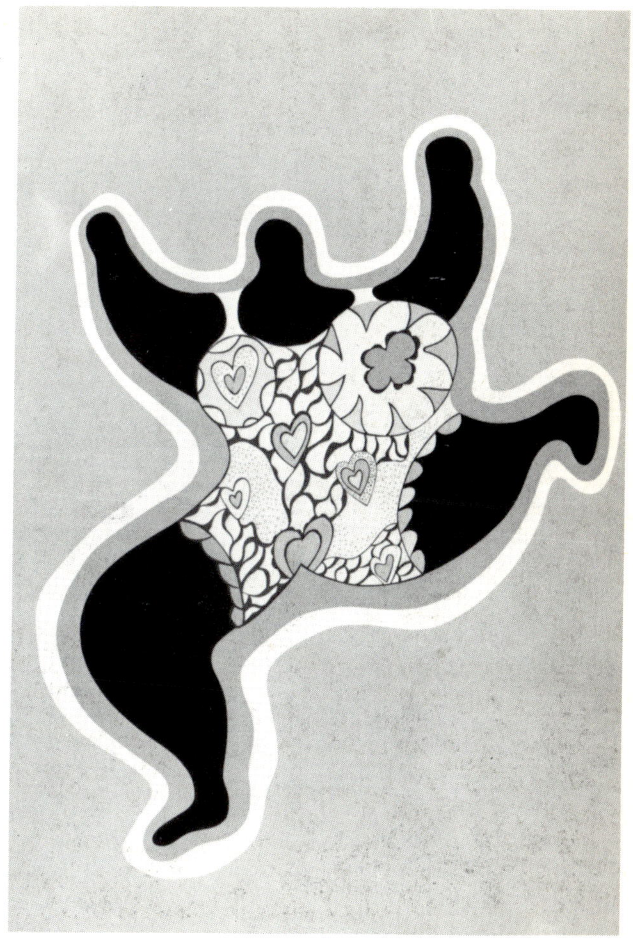

Nicki de Saint-Phalle, from the set Nana Power, *1969. Colour screen print*

In France, Belgium and Switzerland it was not until 1930, that display men, signwriters and decorators started to use screen printing.

The Association of British Silk Screen Printers was founded in 1934.

As for fine art silk screen printing, it is a field that seems to have been entirely in the hands of the Americans. In 1938 Guy Maccoy exhibited a series of original screen prints. Anthony Velonis introduced a large number of American painters to the technique, and the "National Serigraph Society" was founded in 1940. A "Graphic Arts Division" was opened at Princeton University under the aegis of the master-printer Elmer Adler; exhibitions were organized, through which many an American painter-serigrapher became known: Harry Shockler, Leonard Pytlak, Hy Warsager, Edward Landon, Sol Wilson, Max A. Cohn, Mary Van Blarcom, Louise A. Freedman, Doris Meltzer, Henry Mark, Mervin Jules, Ruth Gikow and many others. It was at about this time, too, that Carl Zigrosser of the Philadelphia Museum of Fine Arts coined the word "serigraph", which he defined

Eugenio Carmi, Composition, *1969. 9 colour screen print*

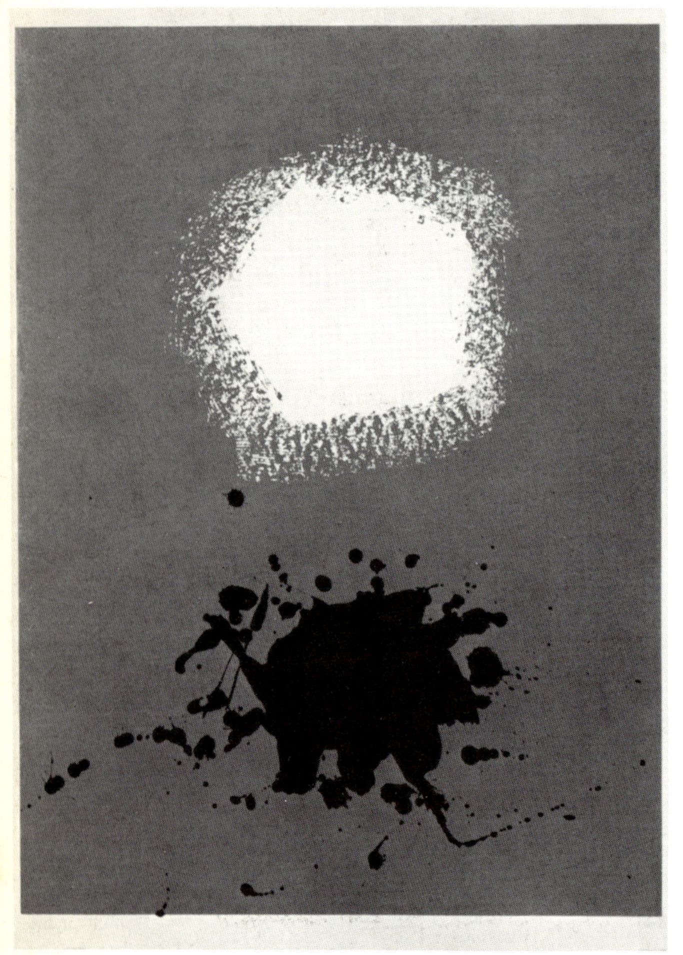

as follows: "A serigraph, or original silk screen print, is one which the artist made after his own design, and for which the artist himself executed the component colour stencils". From this time onwards silk screen was recognized in the United States by critics, collectors and the public alike, as a fine art graphic technique on a level with engraving and lithography. This happy state of affairs was not reached in Europe until twenty years later, as we shall see.

Europe owes a lot to the French artist André Girard. He met Victor Strauss, who for a long while was president of the Research Committee of the American Serigraphy Association, and his wife; they invited him to organize an exhibition in Paris. It was a success, the first of its kind on the continent.

Ranc, then director of the College Estienne and Raymond Haasen, organized courses for artists at that well-known school on the place d'Italie, Paris. At this period Picasso flirted with screen printing,

Adolph Gottlieb, Blues on Green, *1971. Colour screen print*

and Fernand Léger published a suite of prints. Then Chagall, Raoul Dufy and Georges Braque were in turn initiated in the new technique, encouraged by José Mercier.

In industry, Louis Dubuit, supported by his friend Girard, manufactured the first European screen printing machines.

Alas, screen printing, like so many other techniques, owes much of its development to the second world war, in both the fields of printing technique and industrial printing.

The simplicity and light weight of the equipment required and the adaptability of the process, made it the ideal means of printing instructions and references, and markings on helmets, armour, rolling-stock, weapons, planes, etc... Electric circuits printed by a screen process first saw action inside the famous "walky-talky" field radio transmitters.

After the war, surplus material and "demobbed" technicians helped to develop screen printing in industry and graphics;

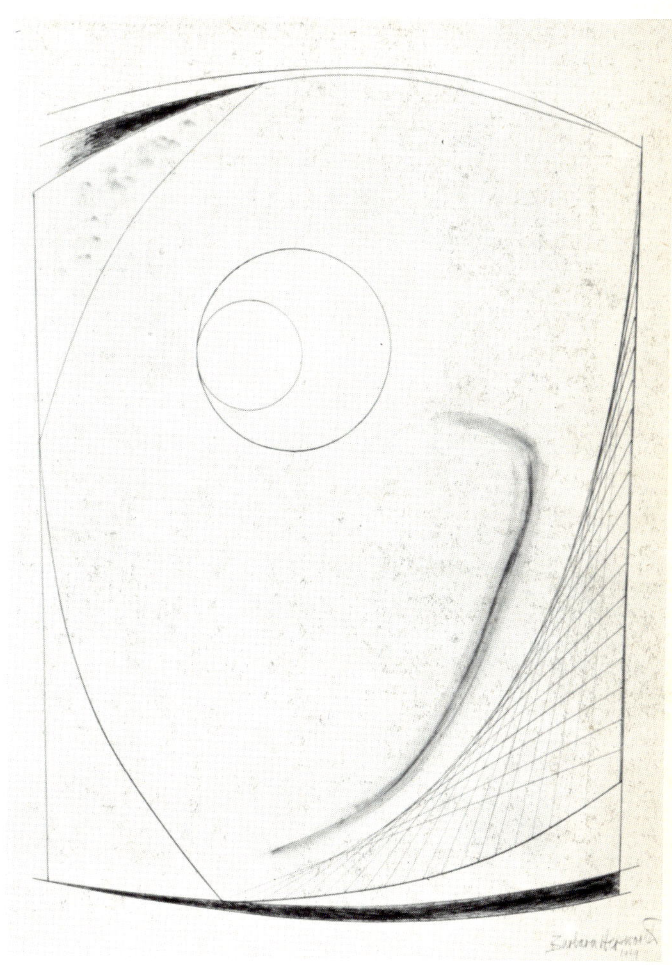

Barbara Hepworth, Winter Solstice, *1969. Colour screen print*

in these fields, during the fifteen years following the war, the use of silk screen became generalized in western Europe.

From 1949 onwards the growth of an important movement could be observed in Belgium, inspired by the Anvers editor, Emil Vanput, who founded the first screen printing reviews in French, Dutch and German.

In France, in 1954, the talented screen printer W. Arcay, presented at the Denise René Gallery, under the patronage of the review *Art d'aujourd'hui*, an exhibition of screen prints of work by artists like Vasarely, Poliakoff, Pilet, Dewasne, Dias, Breuil, Lacasse, Deyrolle, Istrati, Dutrimesco, Bloc, Jacobsen, Leppien, Marie, Raymond.

Germany was by no means lagging behind; a memorable event in that country occured in January 1955, at the "Barmer Kunsthalle", Wuppertal: an exhibition of original serigraphs by Willi Baumeister edited in collaboration with the master screen-printer Poldi Domberger. The exhibition was a sell-out.

Then, from 1960 onwards, screen printing spread to Spain and Portugal, and then towards the East: Yugoslavia first, then Poland, Czechoslovakia, Hungary, the USSR, the Middle East and North Africa, thence to black Africa. From the USA it spread down to Mexico and South America—Brazil and Argentina in particular.

From now on it is no longer possible to talk in terms of "history", we are too close to events. We can, however, note from the artistic point of view, a curious phenomenon: whilst in the United States art screen printing and industrial screen printing develop simultaneously and in harmony, the same cannot be said for continental Europe; in fact, with few exceptions, screen printing has had to be won back to art from the commercial graphics industry. This has caused considerable confusion, which has not yet been quite cleared up, between mass produced silk screen reproductions and "original" screen prints.

Jean Dewasne, from La Longue Marche, *1969. 6 colour screen print*

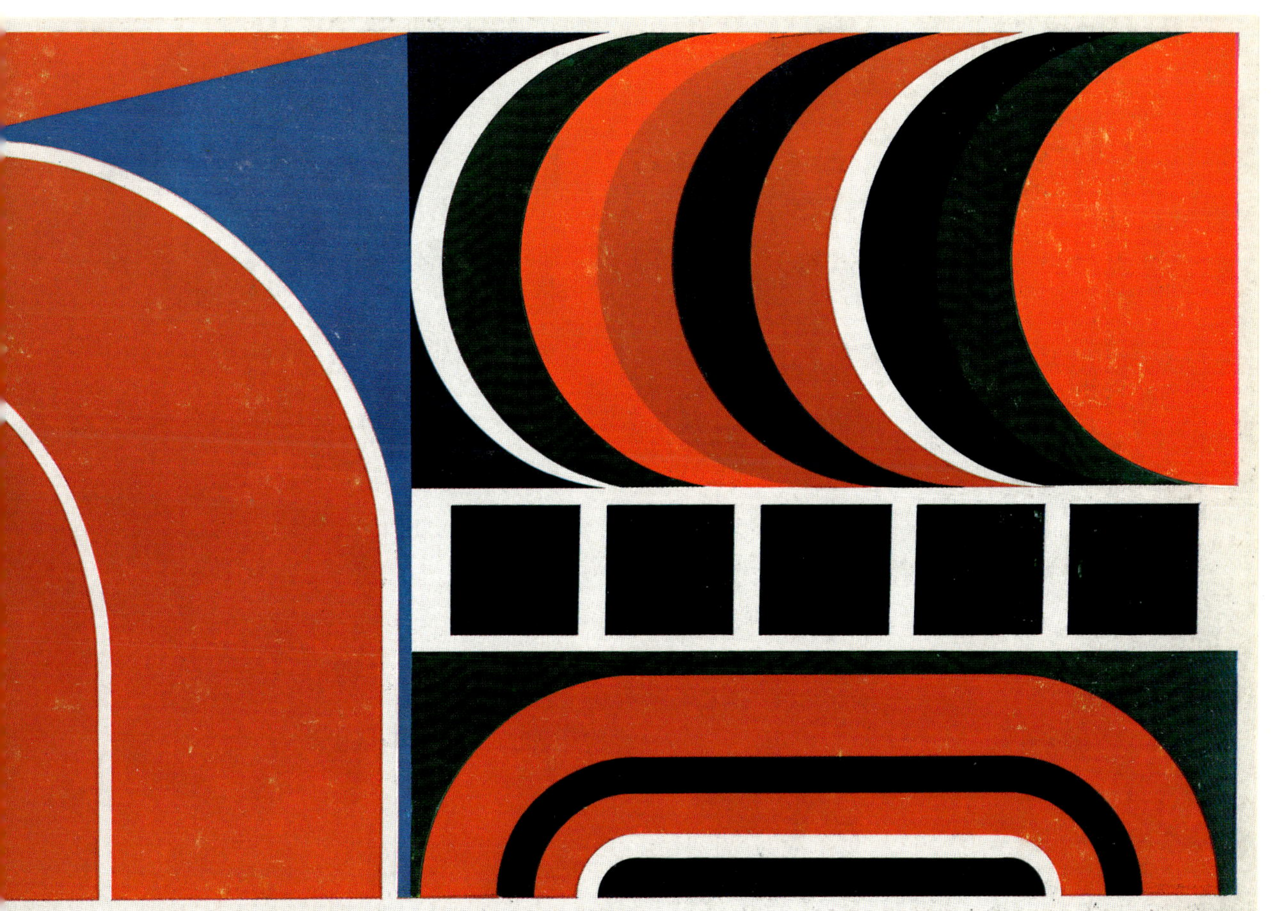

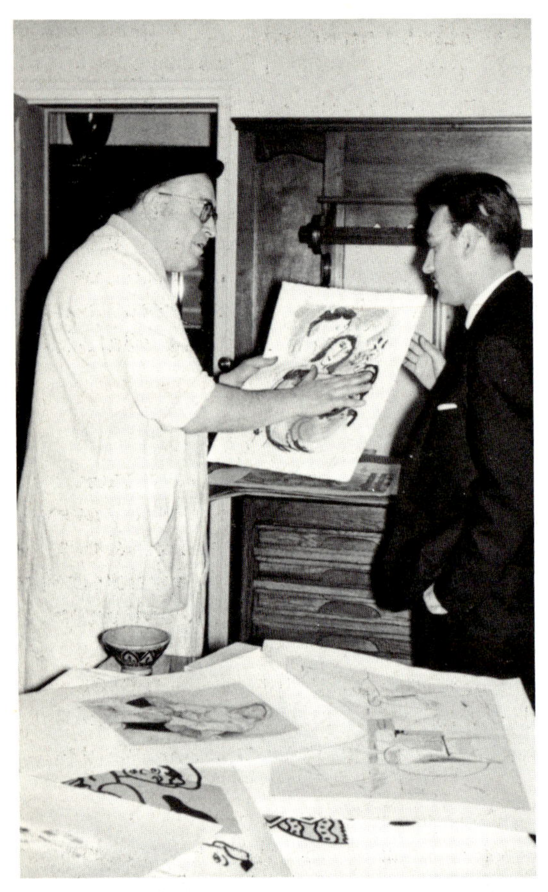

Raymond Haasen working on a copperplate screen print by Chagall

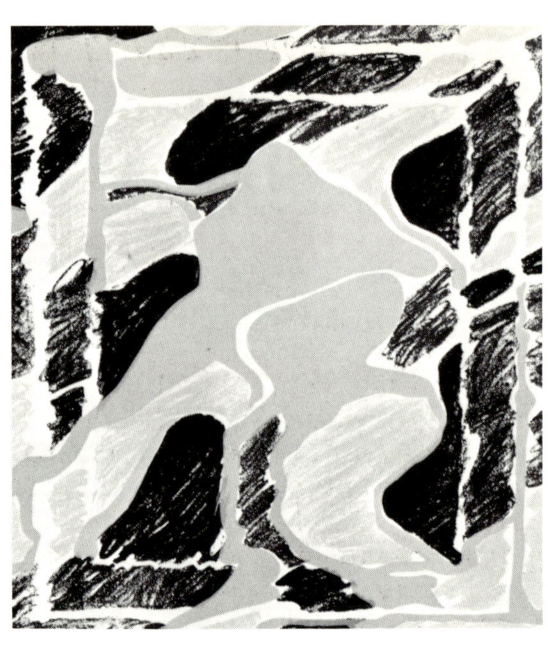

Roland Piché, Essex Landscape, *1971. Colour screen print*

10 FOR COLLECTORS

Whereas in the United States the definition of an "original screen print" has been clear for more than 35 years, a certain amount of confusion still reigns in Europe.

There are really two problems: firstly to get screen printing recognized by art-lovers, editors and artists as a "noble" graphic art on a par with lithography and engraving; secondly, to distinguish between an "original screen print", an "original screen print copy", and a "screen print reproduction".

As far as the first problem is concerned, it is fair to say that in Europe screen printing did finally acquire its "lettres de noblesse" a few years ago.

The second problem could be solved by applying the following definitions:

An "original screen print"

Is a print for which the artist himself executed all the screens for each colour, or the indirect stencils which were transferred to the screens. It must always have been pulled on a manual or semi-manual press under the artist's supervision, in a limited edition, signed and numbered by the artist's own hand. The screens having served for an edition must be effaced and the indirect stencils destroyed.

An "original silk screen copy"

This is usually a screen print executed by a professional printer, by the usual manual techniques, from an artist's original design, but without any direct participation by the artist in the stencil-making and printing. Nevertheless, if the artist is pleased with the final result, he may sign and number the edition. Such editions are occasionally signed jointly by the artist and the printer.

A "screen print reproduction"

This is usually an image reproduced by photomechanical selection of colour based on the principle of trichromatic selection. The printing, which can be of extremely high quality, is usually done with a half-tone screen, although some exceptionally skilled screen printers manage continuous half-tone modulations using a grain effect comparable to lithographic grain. In the latter case, the artist's signature should appear printed in the reproduction. The fact that they may be coutersigned and numbered by the artist in no way saves these prints from being "reproductions".

Signing and numbering

All proofs in an edition of original silk screen prints must, when completed, be numbered; the number of an individual proof should appear, written in the artist's own hand, usually in the bottom left-hand corner of the proof, next to the total number of the edition (11/100 for example). It has been generally accepted that an artist may print an edition consisting of, say, three colour variations of the same design. This must always be apparent in the numbering and the total number of the edition must include all the colour variations.

The first few proofs of an edition to be pulled (1 to 5, for instance), are sometimes

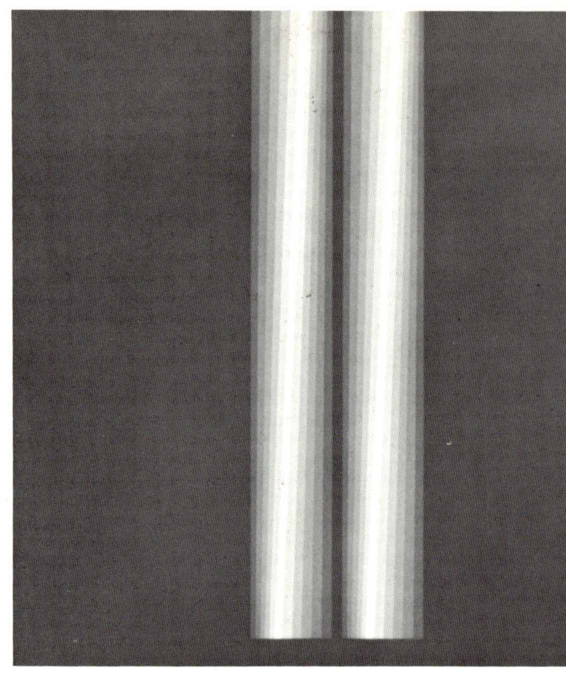

Axel Dick, Doppellicht für Walter, *1971. 7 colour screen print*

Diter Rot, Sicherungen, *1971. Colour screen print* ▷

printed on more luxurious paper than the rest of the edition—to increase their commercial value; this applies particularly to books containing original print illustrations; nevertheless, these proofs are always included in the total number of the edition.

Trial proofs

These are often confused with "over-proofs", with which we shall deal later. Trial proofs are pulled to help work out the exact registration, the correct tonality for each colour and the overall quality of the composition. When these various points have been satisfactorily dealt with, the artist writes his "o.k." in the margin and the edition is ready for printing.

States

States are more or less the same thing as trial proofs; they are certainly "trials", inasmuch as they are used by the artist as a basis for further modification of the screen or colours.

Trial proofs and states are usually destroyed, but many artists and screen printers conserve them by common agreement—but *hors tirage* (i.e. they do not figure in the total number of the edition). As they are unique examples of steps towards the creation of a work, they are often much sought after, even when unsigned.

Over-proofs

These are proofs indentical in every way to the final edition, but pulled over and above the intended total number for the edition, so that the artist can replace any numbered proof which he considers to be of poor quality.

Artist's proofs

Artist's proofs are un-numbered prints from an edition, which are intended for the collections of the artist, editor or printer. Officially their number should not exceed 10 % of the numbered edition. They are marked A.P., and, in principle, are not meant to be sold.

There are other variations which we have already mentioned on previous occasions. *Original multiples*, for example:

Ronald Abram, Composition, *1970. 5 colour screen print*

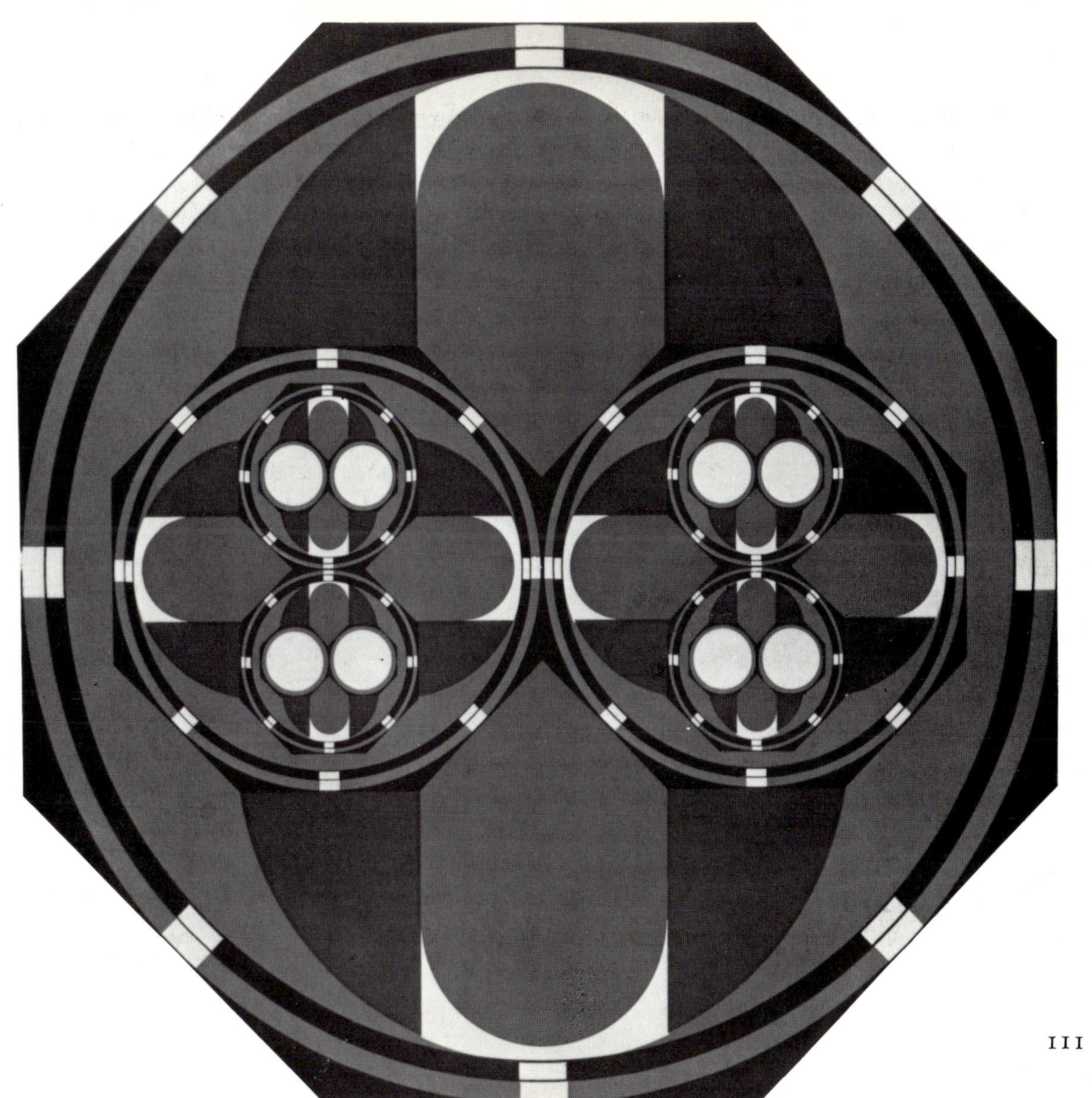

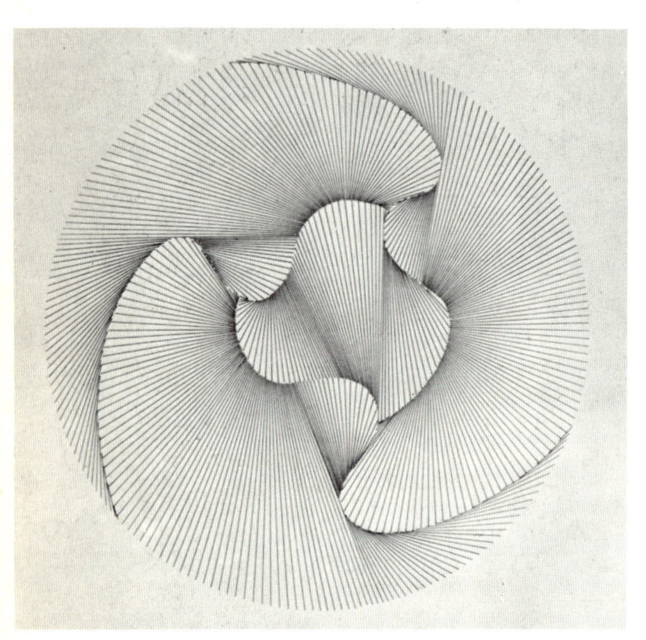

Angel Duarte, Composition, *1971. Black and white screen print*

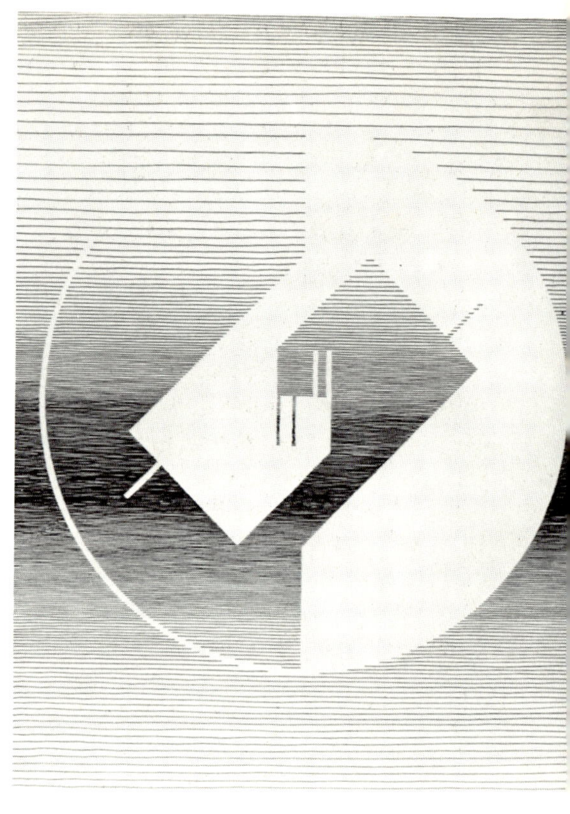

Michel Seuphor, Composition, *1972. Black and white screen print*

these are original screen prints in which the artist has changed one or all of the colours for every proof, without, however, modifying the composition of the work. This can produce 50 or a maximum of 70 variations on a theme. Given the difficult and time-consuming nature of such printing, numbered original multiples are very valuable. *Unedited proofs*, as their name suggests, are proofs from an edition which the artist, for personal reasons, has decided to abandon or interrupt.

Finally there are *monographs*—proofs pulled in only one or two examples, often on other material than paper. This is the case when the artist's intention is to produce a "unique work" using effects that can only be obtained by screen printing, and by no other technique.

Posters fall into a different category. Although Pop Art has boosted them to a level close to original prints, the fact that famous artists have designed them does not alter their value or their aim: they are nearly always printed by mechanical printing processes, usually in runs of over 500 examples, and often of over a thousand. In principle they are never numbered or signed, unless the signature is printed in the composition. They normally bear the name of the printer or the editor. Their commercial value is between ten and a hundred times less than that of an original screen print.

A collector, then, must bear these various factors in mind to avoid unworthy acquisitions. The real value of a work always depends on who signed it, the size of the edition and the quality of the print.

GLOSSARY OF TECHNICAL TERMS

Base. Part of the printing table on which the sheet of paper is placed for printing.

Block-out. Direct stencil technique on the screen. The meshes are obstructed around the design to be printed.

Capillarity. Physical property of fluids which causes them to adhere to solid surfaces with which they are in contact. In silk screen, the way ink adheres to the screen fabric when passing through it.

Clearance (or off-contact). Distance between the lower surface of the screen and the sheet of paper to be printed; it can vary between 1 and 5 mm.

Counter-squeegees. Mobile metal or plastic scraper which inks up the screen in its raised position, causing flood-coating.

Developing. Both direct and indirect photo stencils are developed in water which washes away parts of the light-sensitive film or emulsion which have not been hardened by exposure to ultra-violet light.

Direct and indirect stencils. In the direct method of photochemical stencilling, the whole of the screen is coated with a light-sensitive emulsion and exposed directly. In the indirect method a film is sensitized, exposed and developed away from the screen, then transferred to the mesh afterwards.

Edge. Part of the squeegee blade which is in direct contact with the screen mesh during squeegeeing. The quality of the print depends also on a good edge.

Expanded plastics. Sheet plastics of varying thicknesses containing a high percentage of air. The best known are rigid expanded polystyrene and flexible polyurethane foam.

Exposure. Screens and films, partially protected by transparent positives are exposed to a strongly actinic light source.

Flocking. Short chaff of fabric fibres projected by spray or by electrostatic means onto printed areas of adhesive.

Flood-coating. Inking up of the screen in its raised position. It can be carried out by hand using the squeegee, or mechanically using a metal or plastic counter-squeegee.

Frame. Fabric is stretched on a wood or metal frame to make up the "screen".

Ghost images. If a screen has been poorly cleaned after a previous printing, remaining ink or emulsion cause a faint image of the previous colour to haunt the printer while he pulls the next colour.

Good corner. The corner of a sheet of printing paper which is cut to an accurate right angle. It is placed against the stops or guides during printing to make sure of precise registration.

Guides. Three thin strips of plastic or metal which are fixed to the printing base, usually two at the bottom and one on the side, against which the sheet of paper is placed during printing.

Half-tones. Un-uniform areas of colour containing graduations of the same colour. They are achieved in screen printing using special techniques.

Half-tone screen. A transparent plate ruled with lines of screen dots, used to reproduce half-tones in photo engraving.

Hand-cut stencils. Manual stencilling technique in which a special film is cut with a scalpel away from the screen, then stripped and transferred to the mesh chemically.

Hinges. Attach the screen to the printing base and allow it to be raised or to fall onto the sheet of printing paper.

Kodatrace. Clear acetate tracing film dulled on one side, drawn on with brush or pen using opaque gouache or India ink to make the transparent positive.

Lithfilms. High-contrast films used for making transparent positives photographically.

Litho crayon. Manufactured in various degrees of hardness, it can either be used to draw directly on the screen to obtain grainy half-tone effects, or dissolved and applied in liquid form with a brush.

Litho ink. Used like litho crayon to fill the positive areas of the design on the screen. These are later dissolved and become the openings through which the ink passes. Also known as *tusche.*

Masking tape. Adhesive crepe paper often used to line the inside edges of the screen to prevent ink from seeping between the fabric and the frame.

Mesh. Finely woven fabric which is stretched across the screen frame. The word *mesh* can also be applied to an individual fibre in a fabric, or even to an aperture in the weave.

Mesh count. The number of warp threads that cross an inch of weft thread in a fabric.

Newsprint. Cheap, poor quality paper used to pull waste proofs until the screen is properly inked up.

"O.K.". The artist writes his "O.K." in the margin of the most successful trial proof and signs it. The printing of the edition can now be commenced.

Pool. An amount of ink taken from the *well* in the border of the screen with the squeegee and pulled across the mesh.

Pull (or squeegeeing). The action of printing in silk screen.

Registration. The precise position which a colour must occupy on every sheet of paper in an edition in relation to every other colour and the edges of the sheet.

Registration crosses. 2 or 4 very fine crosses ruled in the margin of a master sketch permitting the various colours to be registered in relation to each other. They are effaced from the screen when trial proofs have been pulled.

Retouching gouache. An opaque gouache, usually brown, used exclusively to retouch transparent positives

Saw-edged profile. An effect noticeable on a print pulled from a design drawn directly on the screen or obtained photographically on a screen with too small a mesh count: the emulsion or stopping-out liquid (filler) follows the structure of the mesh resulting in a sort of "saw-tooth" effect instead of a straight line.

Scalpel (or cutter). Extremely sharp blade used for cutting hand-cut stencils and preparing transparent positives or "Rubylith" films.

Screen. Basically a frame with a fine woven fabric stretched on it. The fabric is selectively obstructed to prevent ink from passing through it, and thus becomes a stencil.

Self-stretching frame. Frame equipped with a mechanical or pneumatic stretching mechanism which provides an evenly stretched fabric.

Serigraph. Name coined for silk screen prints by Carl Zigrosser, Curator of Prints at Philadelphia Museum of Art, when screens are made by the artist.

Seroid. Latex-based ink used for painting a positive design directly on the screen.

Snap-up. How the ink leaves the mesh as soon as the squeegee has passed.

Squeegee. Rubber or synthetic blade set in a wood or metal handle used to push ink across and through the screen.

Squeegee angle. The angle at which the squeegee is held while being pushed or pulled across the screen. Usually between 35° and 85°.

Stencilling. The act of obstructing certain areas of the mesh on a screen.

Stepped profile. See *Saw-edged profile.*

Stopping-out liquid (or filler). Liquid emulsion, usually cellulose or water-based. Used to obstruct the mesh in certain manual techniques, or to fill holes or faults in other stencilling techniques.

Stops. See *Guides.*

Stretching machines. Pneumatic or mechanical machines for stretching the fabric before fixing it on a frame to constitute the screen.

Stripping. In hand-cut stencils the action of peeling from their backing with the help of the scalpel, the areas of film corresponding to the parts of the image which are intended to print. For photo-chemical stencils see *developing.*

Temporary backing (-sheet). The transparent layer of hand-cut or photo stencil sheets which is stripped off when the film itself has been transferred to the screen.

Transparent positive. A transparent sheet, parts of which are made opaque by manual or photographic means. The opaque areas correspond to printing parts of the image, the transparent areas to obstructed mesh on the screen.

Trichromatic printing. Screen printing with the three primary printing ink colours (yellow, magenta, cyan-blue), which are themselves complementary to the primary colours of light (red, blue and green). With trichromatic printing, it is theoretically possible to reproduce extremely faithfully any full-colour picture, with or without half-tones; the colours are selected by photographic means.

Tusche. See *Litho ink.*

Vacuum table. The most popular printing base: it is pierced with small holes leading to an air-tight box. A partial vacuum is created in the box at the moment of printing, which holds the sheet of paper firmly in place during the pull.

Well. A reservoir of ink kept in the water-tight border of the screen round the image.

SELECT BIBLIOGRAPHY

Harry Shokler, *Artist's Manual for Silk Screen Print Making*. New York, 1940

Albert Kosloff, *Screen Process Printing*. Cincinnati, 1950

Igor Pruzan, *L'Ecran de Soie*. 2nd edition. Paris, 1950

Albert Kosloff, *Photographic Screen Process Printing*. Cincinnati, 1955

Michel Caza, *Les Techniques de la Sérigraphie*. 2nd edition. Paris, 1968

Articles

Le Tamis, Nº 10, October 1953

Le Sérigraphe, No. 5, November 1954

Le Tamis, No. 12, December, 1959

Le Tamis, No. 12, December , 1961

Le Tamis, No. 4-5, April-May, 1963

Décoration-PLV-Sérigraphie, No. 48, July, 1963

TABLE OF ILLUSTRATIONS

The base and screen 8–12

Dean Meeker working directly on a screen 13

Joe Tilson, *Earth*, 1971. Silk screen and collage, 97.8 × 67.3 cm. ($38^1/_2$ × $26^1/_2$″). Edition of 70. Edited by Marlborough Graphics Ltd. 15

Preparing the fabric and the screen 16–26

Ronald Abram, *Composition*, 1970. 5 colour screen print, 62 × 62 cm. ($24^3/_8$ × $24^3/_8$″). Edition of 110. From the series *Infinitésimal*. Edited by Baal Teshuva 21

Block-out 28–29

Drawing with seroid 30–31

Fernand Léger, *Composition*, 1950–51. 5 colour screen print. Edited by the artist 33

The Mercier method 34–36

Drawing with litho crayon 37

Victor Pasmore, *Variation 4*, 1972. Colour screen print, 91.5 × 61.2 cm. (36 × 24″). Edition of 60. From the set of 7 *Points of Contact: Variations*. Edited by Marlborough Graphics Ltd. 38

Hand-cut stencils 40–44

Jean Baier, *Composition*, 1971. 4 colour screen print, 60 × 60 cm. ($23^5/_8$ × $23^5/_8$″). Edition of 200. From the set of 10 *Situation I*. Edited by Duo d'Art S.A. 45

Direct photo-stencilling 47–48

Indirect photo-stencilling 49–50

Making the transparent positive 51–54

Gianfredo Camesi, *Mouvement 1971*, 1972. Black and white screen print (detail), 59.4 × 84 cm. ($23^3/_8$ × $33^1/_{16}$″). Edition of 50. Edited by Galerie Renée Ziegler 54

The Linstead method 55

Victor Vasarely, *Composition*, 1966. Colour screen print, 70 × 70 cm. ($27^1/_2$ × $27^1/_2$″). Edition of 100 57

Backings and inks 58–63

Putting the screen in position 64–66

Squeegees 67

Registration 68

Clearance 69

Pulling 70–74

Drying racks 75

Yaakov Agam, *La Thora*, 1971. 98 colour screen print, 86 × 106 cm. ($33^{13}/_{16} \times 41^{11}/_{16}$″). Edition of 150. Edited by Editions du XXe Siècle — 77

Daniel Milhaud working directly on a screen — 78

Maxime Deffert signing proofs — 79

R. B. Kitaj, *Bedroom*, 1971. Colour screen print, 65 × 95 cm. ($25^{9}/_{16} \times 37^{3}/_{8}$″). Edition of 70. Edited by Marlborough Graphics Ltd. — 80

String and cut-out card shapes — 82–83

Screen print advertisement — 84

Printing presses — 86–87

Printing "à la lyonnaise" — 88–89

Pulling a screen print on a semi-automatic printing press — 90

Semi-automatic bottle-printing production line — 91

Printed electronic circuit — 91

Marc Baumann, *Les Paons*, 1962. 5 colour seritapestry, 70 × 100 cm. ($27^{1}/_{2} \times 39^{5}/_{16}$″). Edition of 200. Edited by Atelier Baumann — 93

Detail of a Chinese screen — 94

Lola Fernandez, *Composition*, 1972. 5 colour screen print, 102 × 73 cm. ($40^{1}/_{8} \times 28^{11}/_{16}$″). Edition of 50. Edited by the artist — 95

R. B. Kitaj, *Immortal Portraits,* 1972. Colour screen print, 71.7 × 114.2 cm. ($28^{3}/_{16} \times 44^{15}/_{16}$″). Edition of 70. Edited by Marlborough Graphics Ltd. — 97

R. B. Kitaj, *Outlying London district I*, 1971. Colour screen print, 107.5 × 66 cm. ($42^{5}/_{16} \times 25^{9}/_{16}$″). Edition of 70. Edited by Marlborough Graphics Ltd. — 97

Gérald Ducimetière. *Composition*, 1972. Black and white screen print, 59.4 × 84 cm. ($23^{3}/_{8} \times 33^{1}/_{16}$″). Edition of 50. Edited by the artist — 98

Nicki de Saint-Phalle. From the set of 14 *Nana Power*, 1969. Colour screen print, 56 × 76 cm. ($22 \times 29^{7}/_{8}$″). Edition of 120. Edited by Françoise Esselier — 99

Eugenio Carmi, *Composition*, 1969. 9 colour screen print, 56 × 76 cm. ($22 \times 29^{7}/_{8}$″). Edition of 110. Edited by La Tortue — 101

Adolf Gottlieb, *Blues on Green*, 1971. 3 colour screen print, 83.5 × 65.7 cm. ($32^{13}/_{16} \times 25^{13}/_{16}$″). Edition of 150. Edited by Marlborough Graphics Ltd. — 102

Barbara Hepworth, *Winter Solstice*, 1969. Colour screen print, 78 × 58 cm. ($30^{11}/_{16} \times 22^{13}/_{16}$″). Edition of 60. From the set of 12 *Opposing Forms*. Edited by Marlborough Graphics Ltd. — 103

Jean Dewasne. From the set of 14 *La Longue Marche*, 1969. 6 colour screen print, 49 × 74 cm. ($19^{5}/_{16} \times 29^{1}/_{8}$″). Edition of 110. Edited by Galerie Lahumière — 105

Raymond Haasen working on a copperplate screen print by Chagall — 106

Roland Piché, *Essex Landscape*, 1971 (detail). Colour screen print, 103 × 70.2 cm. ($40^1/_2 \times 27^5/_8$"). Edition of 70. Edited by Marlborough Graphics Ltd. 106

Axel Dick, *Doppellicht für Walter*, 1971. 7 colour screen print, 70 × 70 cm. ($27^1/_2 \times 27^1/_2$"). Edition of 100. Edited by Art in Progress 108

Diter Rot, *Sicherungen*, 1971. Colour screen print, 51 × 73 cm. ($20^1/_{16} \times 28^{11}/_{16}$"). Edition of 50. Edited by Galerie Renée Ziegler 109

Ronald Abram, *Composition*, 1970. 5 colour screen print, 62 × 62 cm. ($24^3/_8 \times 24^3/_8$"). Edition of 110. From the series *Infinitésimal*. Edited by Baal Teshuva 111

Angel Duarte, *Composition*, 1971. Black and white screen print, 60 × 60 cm. ($23^5/_8 \times 23^5/_8$"). Edition of 200. From the set of 10 *Situation I*. Edited by Duo d'Art S.A. 112

Michel Seuphor, *Composition*, 1972. Black and white screen print, 84 × 59.4 cm. ($33^1/_{16} \times 23^3/_8$"). Edition of 100. Edited by the White Gallery 112

PHOTOGRAPHIC CREDITS

Atelier Baumann S.A., Orgeval: p. 88, 89.
Atelier Michel Caza, Franconville, photo Claude Corniot: p. 2, 5, 8, 10, 11, 12, 16, 24, 25, 26, 28, 29, 30, 31, 32, 37, 40, 41, 42, 43, 44, 47, 48, 49, 50, 51, 52, 53, 58, 60, 63, 66, 67, 68, 69, 70, 71, 72, 73, 74, 75, 78, 79, 82, 83, 86.
Michel Caza, Paris: p. 13, 54 (1), 106 (1).
Marlborough Graphics Ltd, London: p. 15, 38, 80, 97, 102, 103, 106 (2).
Photo Raymond Asseo, Geneva: cover, p. 23, 45, 54 (2), 57, 64, 65, 84, 87, 91, 95, 97, 98, 99, 108, 109, 111, 112.
Photo Henry Cohen, Paris: p. 21, 61, 77, 93, 101, 105.
Photo Gilbert Dupuis: p. 94.
Photo Dubuit, Paris: p. 91.
Photo Duo d'Art: p. 90.
Photo Heri, Soleure: p. 34, 35-36.
Société Suisse de Tissage de Soies à bluter S.A., Thal (Switzerland): p. 18, 19, 22.

The publishers wish to express their thanks to those who helped work on the preparation of this book; in particular members of the atelier Michel Caza, Franconville, and Daniel Staudhammer at the atelier Duo d'Art, Geneva, who made their workshops available for the technical photography, also José Mercier, Soleure, and Arthur Jobin, Ecublens.
English version by Julian Snelling and Claude Namy.

Printed in Switzerland